GW00776611

Leap Castle

Leap Castle

A PLACE AND ITS PEOPLE

Marigold
Freeman-Attwood

MICHAEL RUSSELL

First published in Great Britain 2001
by Michael Russell (Publishing) Ltd
Wilby Hall, Wilby, Norwich NR16 2JP

Typeset by Waveney Typesetters
Wymondham, Norfolk
Printed and bound in Great Britain
by Biddles Ltd, Guildford and King's Lynn

ISBN 0 85955 263 2

Dedicated to the late Peter Bartlett, who rescued Leap,
and to Seán Ryan, who continues to revive it.

Let no one say the Past is dead.
The Past is all about us, and within.

OODGEROO NOONUCCAL (KATH WALKER)
Australia's first published
Aboriginal poet

Contents

Author's Note

In this book I have tried to mind how I go, treading gratefully on territory explored by historians and other academics who have been kind enough to allow me to enter it. I have sat in no libraries and consulted no primary sources other than the sparse flotsam washed up during house clearances of departed relations. Ours was not a family that kept records, and whatever the Darbys of Leap had in their archive was burned. Wherever possible, I have asked permission from those whose work I have pillaged, and in all cases I have given them thankful recognition. Lacking the skills to do otherwise, I am guilty of stumbling about in other people's painfully acquired research material, thereby assuming a fancy-dress mantle of learning. To those whom I have inadvertantly misrepresented, I offer my sincere apologies.

Acknowledgements

My heartfelt thanks are due to the following, for their most generous help and advice: Anne Callanan, José Croft, George Cunningham, Kari Dill, Professor Laurence Dreyfus, Ken Faris, John Feehan, Dr Elizabeth FitzPatrick, Elizabeth Foster, Professor Roy Foster, Henrietta Freeman-Attwood, Jonathan Freeman-Attwood, Warren Freeman-Attwood, George Gossip, Théa Gray, Noel Guerin, Rosemary Harley, Heather Hilliard, Margaret Hogan, Professor Rolf Loeber, Dr Patrick Melvin, the late John Minchin, Professor P. McNair, Nigel Nicolson, P. K. Page, Fiona Piddock (Librarian to Lincoln College, Oxford), the Revd John Reynolds, Alison Rosse, Alexandra Ruffel, Seán Ryan, His Honour Judge Robert Smyth, Tony and Carmel Swayne, Harry Wedderburn, Sarah Wedderburn, Richard and the Revd Janet White-Spunner.

Introduction

Leap. It is pronounced 'Lepp'. The very word has a spring in it. The full latter-day title of the Irish home of my ancestors is The Leap Castle, as witnessed by my grandmother's calling card, one of a few evocative articles still to be found in the morocco-leather jewellery box given to her (so says the carefully preserved fragment of card within) by her mother on 20 November 1882, when she would have been nearly fifteen years old.

On first revisiting Leap after more than sixty years, it seemed oddly small yet redolent of menace. Re-encountered on a grey, drizzly day in spring, the barely breathing ruin seemed to consist only of its outer walls. Some lines of the poet Ralph Hodgson ran through my head:

> See, an old, unhappy bull
> Sick in mind and body both,
> Slouching in the undergrowth...
>
> Pity him, this fallen chief,
> All his splendour, all his strength,
> All his body's breadth and length
> Dwindled down with shame and grief....

'Dwindled down with shame and grief.' I did not go through the castle gateway, although there was smoke rising from the gatehouse chimney. I needed to stay for the time being at a respectful distance. I drove round, past the little Protestant church at nearby Aghancon, and gazed across a couple of improbably green fields to where the east side of the castle still fixed its vanquished glare over the valley it had once subjugated and guarded. It dominated the skyline, not by its size but by its faint, unextinguished air of overlordship. Rain started. It fell in silvery rods, like a Japanese woodcut. I envisaged it cross-hatched by horizontal showers of bright arrows from the mean slits in the keep. The scene blurred; the imagination went into overdrive. I got out of the car and walked across to the church, built in 1786. No nonsense there. Gothic in style, yet utterly simple, functional and unadorned, it had the look of a governess, determined that her charges should toe the line. St Bernard, so mistrustful of excess, would have approved of its modest bell tower and plain lines. My grandfather, Jonathan Darby, liked it too; his four surviving children were baptised there and his two elder daughters joined their husbands at its altar in holy matrimony. His body lies in the family vault in the grassy churchyard, with that of his baby son, Jonathan Richard.

Inevitably, in this narrative, people and places will intermingle, charging each other with the energies that each emanates. People, places and the traces of a long past form part of one whole. Stones and bones; blood, battles and bogies; heroes, heroines, humanitarians, despots and downright villains leave their mark on the ambience of the place, even now, as loving, skilled hands lift the castle up from where, at the hands of its desecrators, it fell in upon its own foundations, only a mere shell surviving to contain its faintly beating heart. Leap is coming to life again. On that first encounter, I saw none of this renaissance. I saw only sadness and decay.

On the following morning, I was invited to visit Leap by its most recent owner, the musician, Seán Ryan. 'Come about eleven,' he said over the telephone, 'there'll be a few things going on, but just walk in.' A few things going on! Irishmen are not noted for understatement, and I have to conclude that what hit me amidships was normality to a creative artist and champion of the arts going about his daily business. It still rained. The place, close up, looked sadder, mouldier than ever, like an old film star met in a lift. I felt cold, discouraged, almost stifling in a miasma of decay. Then I pushed open the neo-Gothic front door and went in.

The great hall of the keep was flooded by light, thronged with intent, bustling people. 'Now then, let's do it once more; this time we'll be recording,' said a brisk voice. There, bathed in photographers' spotlights, I saw a sea of young faces, alert and concentrated. A pause, a raised baton, and then, soaring out into the bare grey space and in perfect tune came the folk song 'She Moved through the Fair', unaccompanied, pure as a waterfall. 'Good', said the dark girl with the baton, 'we'll take a break'; and I came to, aware, now, of a smell of wet garments, and of a young woman struggling to carry a camcorder up a narrow stone staircase. I put out my hands to take some of the weight. 'I'm Marigold', I said; 'd'you mind my being here?' 'Heavens, no!' she replied. She was Sharon. They were a team from Bradford Arts Council, recording the work of children in music and drama.

At the top of the stair was another large room. A log fire blazed. Boys and girls, streaming in from several directions, were noisily gathering round a large table, unwrapping sandwiches and opening cans of drink. Somebody shushed them, as sounds of music came from another part of the upstairs space. I looked through, and there was Seán Ryan himself (whom I had met previously) giving lessons on the tin whistle, a traditional Irish instrument of which he is a famous and acclaimed player. The lesson ended. Seán joined us in the big room, a welcoming host. He handed round tumblers of neat Irish whiskey to the Bradford team, to the teachers who accompanied the children, and, happily, to me. It seeped into cold bones, warming them as the music had warmed my spirits. In that rosy glow, the castle seemed to be shaking off the uneasy slumber of three-quarters of a century, stirring into a joyful awakening. It felt wonderful just to be there. Seán explained that he wanted Leap to be not only a home, but also a centre for creative activities, especially local ones, and that these young people were from the Community School in Birr. He added that this upper room was in fact a restoration of what had originally been there, before the floor was removed and a gallery substituted, overhanging the hall below.

Aglow with drink, firelight, friendly talk, I studied the faces of the children, aged about thirteen upwards, as they fooled around over their lunch. They were a lovely group, fine-featured in most cases, but what struck me particularly was a kind of serenity of expression, combined with openness, reminiscent of pre-Raphaelite paintings. One girl could have been Guinevere. I had spotted something akin to this in the quality of their singing: a dark purity of tone, quite unlike the voices of English children, heard so often at school concerts. Was this to do with living in what the French tourist pamphlet described as *le coeur tranquil d'Irlande*? It has been far from tranquil in the past, God knows, and that very morning the children had been re-enacting scenes from the Potato Famine of 1845–51, but wounds, here at least, seemed to have healed at long last. No doubt these young people were prey to the uncertainties and fears that assail all of us at that age, but there was, all the same, less evidence of wariness and strain than I have observed recently in the faces of many English children.

Once more, at my request, the choir sang 'She Moved through the Fair'. It may have been the drink, but I felt that no bad vibrations could contend with the grave beauty of that traditional tune. Jerry Crawford, the sound recordist, sent me a tape of it later and, whenever I play it, it dispels any gloomy or fearful reaction I may have in my thoughts of

Leap. That day, I saw what I had failed to spot from the outside, in the dreary mist; that The Leap Castle, with a spring in its name, is on its way to a bright future.

I
Blowing on the Embers

Where do I begin? Chronology is the backbone of a story but I doubt if even the most uncompromisingly fundamentalist Christian would countenance the idea of God starting, in the case of the vertebrates, with the backbones, and carrying on from there. Creation is not like that, nor is re-creation the same process as recording. A story must start with a stirring of the life force, and how you tell it depends on who and where you are.

There are days when the storyteller sees only connections, as if he or she were part of the net overhanging the mythical palace of the Indian god, Indra, where every jewelled knot reflects every other, so that cause and effect become dynamic. This mode of seeing is of course as capable of distortion as the one that catches only the distinctness of separate detail; one has to try to focus the eye of the mind so that it encompasses both of these perspectives. Old age bestows the additional blessing of recognising the slow movement; the turning of the great wheels that set in motion the smaller ones, right down to tiny discs, like the miniscule watch parts reputedly found in the dungeons of Leap. The observer must stand somewhere in the middle of the gyrations, looking both ways, like Janus, the Roman god with two faces. I have tried to do this in writing the story of Leap Castle and the people who lived there: cause and effect are partners in a dance down the ages.

To the Princes of Ely O'Carroll, who built the castle at about the end of the fifteenth century and lived in it for over 150 years, Leap was both a fortress and a home. From time to time it was knocked about by enemies but it was never made uninhabitable. The O'Carrolls' successors and putative descendants, the Darbys of Leap, took a pride in their new property. They enhanced the building with tasteful additions during their long occupation of Leap, while succeeding generations preserved and restored the original parts. By the start of the twentieth century, the castle was regarded as a national monument. It had stood for well over 300 years when the end came on 30 July 1922. Consumed by fire the old place seemingly died, and with it perished a part of the last king of the castle, my grandfather, Jonathan Charles Darby of Leap.

What of the people who lived at Leap for so long, whose destiny was intertwined with the fortress and the land? I have tried to trace the backbone of this composite being, bowing to the necessity of a chronological approach. From time to time I have let conjecture out of its kennel to give my ancestors, the supposed and the proven ones, a run for their money (all in keeping with my vision of re-creation). The last generation of my family to live there are all dead. From their days, only the fading photographs and a few evocative possessions remain, as well as the tales they told us, the snippets of history, the wealth of legend and fable that furnished their own past and, perhaps most interesting of all, our notions of who they were.

We, the ageing children of that last family to call it home, cherish these fragments of matter and of memory, particularly the latter. Each of us is a separate repository of anecdotes about Leap's final years of occupancy. Needless to say, the stories do not always tally. Did my mother and her siblings really tip their governess out of a dog-cart to settle a bet about whether or not she wore a wig? And did Miss Alice Harty, if indeed it was she, report this to her illustrious conductor/composer brother, Sir Hamilton? Did Grandfather really hurl his plate of raspberry fool at the dining-room wall to indicate the exact colour he wished it to be painted? Did the dogs bark every evening, half an hour before midnight, and the ghosts walk, severally, in due season, observed by Milly Darby, my novelist grandmother? Would no foxhound ever cross the threshold of the Leap Demesne, and did its most famous ghost, the Elemental, truly stalk the battlements on the night of the great conflagration in 1922? Now we just say that we shall never know. We knew then, as listening children, while we still trailed our "clouds of glory". Legend planted in a child's mind masquerades there as a kind of truth for evermore, however doggedly the brain tries to refute it. The same is probably true of historical consciousness in the minds of those of us with a taste for the picturesque; we are inherently biased. Much of what is related hereafter can be thus accounted for or is non-verifiable for more respectable reasons, like an absence of facts.

There can be no account of the fortunes of Leap and the activities of the O'Carrolls and Darbys that does not connect them with the historical events of the time, and it was not until I applied myself to a study, albeit cursory, of the history of Ireland that I realised why it was not taught in English schools in my day. In the case of England's treatment of the Irish, from the time of the Anglo-Norman invasions in the mid-twelfth century onwards, we can only hope with mounting horror that they knew not what they did. Even when there is evidence of a desire to deal fairly with internal disputes during the times when England held precarious sway over the island, that often appears to be only a part of the invaders' attempt to obtain total control, which in the end they did. Such so-called civilising influences as the English brought to that country, were, until well into the eighteenth century, usually imposed with such improbity as to render the cost immeasurably too great. Ends can seldom have been so cruelly unjustified by means. The one redeeming feature of England's dealings with Ireland is that, from Anglo-Norman times on, those who settled there became, with time, as much influenced as influential, bringing, through intermarriage and cultural mixing, breadth to a society previously remarkable for depth, and themselves receiving the fruits of that profundity. The Ireland of today testifies to this curious benefit.

The Leap Castle, or just Leap, as it was regularly referred to by the family, always loomed large in my consciousness. That stark monosyllable was scary in itself. I connected it with the springing leopard, with leprosy, and later with the terrifying image of a young lover leaping, or lepping, as the Irish say, from the battlements – one of the many 'origins' of the name. Often I fell with him in my dreams, to wake with a start just before I hit the rocks below. I wished the castle was called Castle Rising, the only one I had been in. My mother had two watercolours of Leap as it had been in her childhood. The artist had painted the building a warm beige and surrounded it with the trees and flowers of a well-kept garden, but the menace of the great keep persisted; a leopard garlanded is not a leopard tamed. I was thrilled and appalled to be part of its reality.

Sometimes, in a rare moment of relaxation, after Sunday lunch, for instance, as the Cona coffee machine hissed and gobbled over the blue flame that activated it, my mother would tell us about Leap. With the verve of the natural storyteller she would recall the adventures of her life there – the legends, the hauntings, her mother's intense involvement with the spirits, her father's scornful dismissal of them. Sometimes she mentioned the burning, briefly, without her customary dramatic turn of phrase.

I was terrified of fire. There was a book in the drawing room with a picture of someone being burnt at the stake. This had a horrible fascination. I hid the book deep under the sofa, returning to it secretly from time to time for the thrill it gave me. Once I could read fluently I was drawn to poetry, and one day discovered a poem that fed my morbid addiction to fear, 'The Hound of Heaven' by Francis Thompson. 'I fled Him down the arches of the years' invoked the image of a slavering fox-hound chasing me down the corridors of Leap, where flames licked the pointed doorways. I became a secretive, baffling child, irritating to my forthright mother, puzzling to my merry, sporting father. Stout, timid and given to tears, I can see that I was not a very rewarding member of the family.

Our father died when I was thirteen, and the following summer our mother took us all to Ireland for a holiday. One day we went to Leap. The sun shone and we took a picnic. Our pretty, vivacious Aunt Cis, recently remarried, was there with her step-children, Anne and Robert, as well as several others, and we young ones, quite without the sophistication of our modern counterparts, scrambled up and down the spiral staircase, in and out of the ruins, deaf to the half-hearted admonitions of the grown-ups below. Then someone shouted 'Lunch, children!' and there was a downward clatter and shove to the cold chicken and salad. A greedy child, I nevertheless hung back. Now was my chance to see a ghost. Unlikely, you might suppose, on a hot July morning, but I was undeterred. I lurked, very still, at the top of the spiral stairs, by the chapel doorway. I became porous. 'O ghost, do please come. Please, please appear!' Sure enough, there was a girl, standing by the window. An old child, large as life. I didn't notice what she wore, only that she was like me. 'You are real, aren't you?' I insisted, as she began to fade. She didn't answer, or smile, or anything, so I blew her a kiss and then she vanished. Someone called my name from below. The spell was broken and I was suddenly ravenous.

This vivid memory has set me wondering whether susceptibility to local atmosphere, powered by self-suggestion, does not evoke images in places of special power, which are on the periphery of the mysterious 'real thing'. Or perhaps I could be said to have seen a vision. Time gave substance to the event in my mind. It became as solid a part of the day out as the cold chicken, the strawberries and the loud laughter of the grown-ups, who had wined as well as dined. On the way home in the hot car I pondered on the matter, smelling of dust and grass and chafed by the tight knicker elastic round my sunburnt legs. Perhaps I imagined the whole thing, but I thought I had seen the ghost of a girl, and I never told a soul.

After that first visit, I did not see Leap again for over sixty years, when

I returned to blow on the embers of the past, to try to recall from the distances of long ago the life of the place – its purpose and its people. At the same time, Seán Ryan, with his own skilled hands, places stone upon stone, restoring the fabric, each stone bringing nearer the day when the castle will once more be a family home; a place with a future.

2
The O'Carrolls

PART ONE: BEFORE THE PLANTATION

The story of Leap must begin with an account of the O'Carrolls of Ely who, with the exception of a period when it may have been the home of the O'Bannons, owned it and its lands, in the centre of Ireland, for over a century and a half. We must go back in history to see the sort of people they were and to get an idea of the world they lived in before and during their occupation of the castle. We cannot be certain who owned it if, as some experts believe, it existed in an earlier form, but the present castle was an O'Carroll stronghold from the end of the fifteenth century or perhaps a little later.

The Anglo-Norman invasions of Ireland in the second half of the twelfth century, a hundred years or so after William the Conqueror took England, heralded the start of continual attempts by the English to annexe Ireland as a part of Britain. Before that time Ireland was a land entirely composed of principalities, or septs, as they were called, self-governing and each ruled by a patriarchal chieftain with the title of Prince. The O'Carrolls, whose proper Gaelic name was O Cearbhaill, were fierce and bellicose, their name derived from Cearbhall, son of the ancient King of Munster who ruled Ely in the ninth century. They were, therefore, people of Munster by early tradition, grouped with the genealogies of that territory and not to be confused with two other early medieval monarchies of the same name. The area they inhabited was that part of the Irish Midlands that is today south County Offaly and north County Tipperary, traversed by the main route from the Midlands to Dublin, called the *Slighe Dhala*.

Although the sept bore their name, these O'Carrolls were what we might call an extended family, for there were, under the dominion of O'Carroll, Prince of Ely, other tribes such as the O'Bannons, with their own aristocratic inheritance, occupying their own clan territories within the principality. In times of trouble they would band together, although in-fighting was not unknown.

The boundaries of Ely were fluid to say the least, as neighbouring tribes were constantly endeavouring to extend their own land, but the warlike O'Carrolls were not often defeated, earning for themselves, in bardic tradition, the sobriquet of 'the O'Carrolls of the reddened spears'. The bard, highly respected and venerated, would in fact have been a propagandist in the pay of the chief, but nevertheless this reputation must have been intimidating for others with ambitions for territorial aggrandisement. They were also dubbed 'Lords to whom stoop the hazelnut trees' and 'the O'Carrolls of the flaxen hair', by the bard O'Heedrin,[1] which makes them sound romantically attractive, but there is every reason to suppose them to have been as rapacious and bloodthirsty as the rest of the inhabitants of Ireland's principalities in those early days. The O'Carrolls were to thwart all attempts at subjugation on the part of their neighbours and of the invading English for several hundred years. The chroniclers could write that at the death of Thady O'Carroll, Prince of Ely, in 1346, he 'had slain or expelled from his patrimony the nations of the Brets, the Milbournes and other English, and had occupied their lands and castles'.[2] His successors, although gradually stripped of their power by English attempts to subdue and colonise the country, were never wholly defeated until Cromwell's troops arrived in 1649.

The Elyans were rumoured to have been a race of giants, which we can take to mean that they were unusually large; not quite the same thing and probably put about by themselves. Their clan emblem was the hawk, a bird associated in mythology with royalty and power and said to be able to outstare the sun. Sometimes the chief would use a stylised picture of a hawk as his signature, which looked, I imagine, rather like the Egyptian symbols carved on the walls of ancient temples. 'Praise to the Hawk!' was one of their battle cries. Some of the chiefs embraced learning, or at any rate promoted culture with zeal, but as a sideline to their primary duty as head of the clan. In this latter capacity they were reminded of their obligations from time to time by the learned men of the tribe, called the Ollamh, who were responsible for compiling the genealogies, updating them, and declaiming them frequently to the ruler to keep him up to the mark. These early tribal genealogies have survived in written form in a great volume called *Senchus Mor,* which means 'Knowledge of Antiquity' and is an invaluable source of information.

1 Died in 1420.
2 *The Annals of Clynn* (1346).

The title of prince, or chief, was not hereditary. Since the clan's main preoccupation was defending its territory and, when the chance arose, grabbing a bit extra in the way of land and livestock from neighbours, the chief would have been chosen for his brain, his brawn and, no doubt, his powers of leadership; not a man to be trifled with and liable to be peremptorily disposed of if proved to be inadequate. I might mention here that the prefix 'O', meaning 'descendant of', in clan names came in during the tenth century. As for first names, a small selection recur frequently, such as (in English) Charles, Mulrony, Thady, Rory, Donough, John, and the Anglo-Norman William, necessitating the use of sobriquets like the One-Eyed, the Pale and the Bearded.

From the beginning of the thirteenth century, the greatest threat to the large and well-defended kingdom of Ely, bounded as it was on all sides by natural barriers of bog, mountain, river and forest, came from a powerful Anglo-Norman neighbouring family, the Butlers. The original oppressor was Theobald Walter. He was the Chief Butler of all Ireland (so called because he had the honour of pouring the king's wine as well as the hazardous responsibility of tasting it), under the newly crowned King John. The Ormond Deeds of 1172–1350 state that the king had made over 'the entire cantred of Elykareul' to his Chief Butler, who was created the Earl of Ormond in 1201, adopting the family name of Butler. That was when the trouble began. His Majesty had underestimated the O'Carrolls. They defied the order, so that in 1306, in Edward II's reign, a servant of the Crown complained to his superior, the local sheriff, that it was quite impossible for him to carry out his duties in 'the March of Elycarewill'.[3] Their chief took orders from no one, and *The Annals of the Four Masters*[4] record that 200 men of Ormond's army were slain in battle by the O'Carrolls in 1315, as the former made one of their many attempts to get the land the king had awarded them. One must, in fairness, admit that the Butlers had reason to feel cheated of their due.

Permanently outraged at this threatened confiscation of their ancient territory, the O'Carrolls continued to ignore the royal decree, and over the succeeding 400-odd years the area, though depleted, was never

3 *Calender of the Justiciary Rolls of Ireland Edward I*, ed. J.Mills, part 2 1305–1307 (London 1914), p. 194.

4 The popular name for *The Annals of the Kingdom of Ireland*. This was compiled by Michael Cleary, a Franciscan monk, and three collaborators between 1632 and 1636 by collating all the ancient manuscripts available to them. The books are unparalleled in Irish literature both as historical documents and as works of art. In 1851 they were published, with a translation and commentary by John O'Donovan. Hereafter referred to as *AFM*.

taken by the Butlers or by any other of its predatory neighbours. The Kildares in particular were a rich and powerful Anglo-Norman family, sometimes friendly but more often out for what they could get, particularly when they could act in the capacity of loyal servants of the Crown. By the late fourteenth and early fifteenth centuries, however, the O'Carroll princes seem to have been sufficiently in control of their territory to apply themselves to matters other than warfare and farming.[5] This was a time of 'Gaelic Resurgence' throughout the land, with colonisation actually on the decline, due to the failure of Richard II's second attempt to subdue the native population, in 1399. It is around this time that the ancestors of the O'Carrolls of Leap begin to form a fascinating backdrop to the activities of those characters who actually lived there.

Thady, Prince of Ely O'Carroll, was a warrior with several other attributes. He was married in the latter part of the fourteenth century, doubtless for political reasons, to Joan Butler, the daughter of the Earl of Ormond, and was, say the Four Masters, 'deservedly a man of great accompt and fame with the professors of poetrye and Musicke of Ireland and Scotland, for his liberality extended towards them and every one of them in generalle'.[6] This picture of a man who recognised the work of individuals, rather than just giving blanket patronage to the arts is intriguing. The Shrine at Roscrea of *The Book of Dimma*, an illuminated medieval manuscript now in the National Museum, was repaired and redecorated at his behest. He presumably selected the artists and craftsmen to carry out this work, and may have made suggestions of his own. I see him standing over them, probably to their irritation. He also became patron of the twelfth-century church at Roscrea, St Cronan's, of which only the west gable, with fine Hiberno-Romanesque carving, still stands. (This ravishing architectural hybrid is emblematic of the invincibility of the Irish identity.) Moreover, the Four Masters tell us that Thady went on pilgrimage to Rome, after which he paid a call on the French court, and then did likewise in England, where he was received by Richard II. Although at that moment the two must have been on fairly cordial terms, the relationship seems later to have gone sour, for in 1395 the Prince of Ely O'Carroll's troops beat an

5 Farming on native Irish properties was mixed, cattle being the most important as a means of wealth, with pigs in wooded areas, such as Ely. By the Middle Ages there was extensive cultivation, especially of oats. The Anglo-Normans introduced systematic agriculture as well as sheep farming and wood clearance.The bard O' Heedrin refers to Ely as 'The land of Cattle'.

6 *AFM*, pp. 791–2.

English army led by the Earl of March, sent by the king to reimpose his authority on both the native inhabitants and the Anglo-Norman colonists – many of whom by this time saw themselves as more Irish than English. Thady was slain by the invading force in 1407.

At the time of this famous man's death, his elder daughter Margaret O'Carroll was seven years old, one of a family of five children. It is not known whether her mother was Joan Butler or one of the two other people with whom her father's name was linked. Of three O'Carroll women who are remembered for their good works, she is the most important. Each, in her own way, was as influential as her husband and deserves to be remembered as a force for good in this story, counter-balancing to some extent the ignoble pursuits of some of the clan.

Margaret was probably about fifteen at the time of her marriage to Charles, the son of Murrough O'Conor, a neighbouring chieftain anxious, no doubt, to ally his realm with that of Ely O'Carroll in the interests of power and security. The O'Conors were by tradition allies of the O'Carrolls and Charles, being himself a warrior and a patron of the arts, had much in common with Thady O'Carroll. This may well have contributed to his successful and long-lasting marriage to Margaret.

Marriages among the Irish nobility at that time were pragmatic contracts, unconnected with the Church and, as in the case of Margaret's father, made for political expediency, with the temporal powers and rights of each to be upheld. This conferred upon the wife an autonomy one would not expect of those days. Margaret was not the subject of her husband – everything else that each possessed was to be shared equally between them. She would, however, have undertaken to tender to her husband 'her will and desire and female act', while he was pledged to give her 'the virile act'.[7] There is a wry psychological insight inherent in the fact that the woman is required to be both willing and enthusiastic in the marriage bed (headaches were presumably out of the question) while it is assumed that this is, in the husband's case, part and parcel of the act.

Each of them would have been fostered out with relations, the grander the better, as children. This was the tradition among the nobility, and it prevailed well into the seventeenth century. The custom, widely practised on the Continent in those days by the nobility and still alive today in a very different form among a small minority of well-to-

7 *Ancient Laws of Ireland, Senchus Mor* (Commissioners for Publishing the Ancient Laws and Institutes of Ireland, London, 1869), vol. 2, p. 347.

do British, appears to have its roots in a common intention. Social prestige and the best possible education? Certainly, and could it be that then, as now, the home environment might be deemed to be too soft for the development of qualities necessary for survival at the top of the heap? You had to be both worldly wise and tough to survive, whether boy or girl, if born into the nobility of the clan. Medieval Irish parents cannot have needed to be available for endless social engagements or free to pursue independent careers. We must give Margaret and Charles the benefit of the doubt, accepting that they sent their seven children away from home for what they saw as their own good. Certainly the arrangement would have made possible the public work that Margaret undertook on her marriage, sharing in the administration of the jointly held estates, and, according to her 1451 obituary,[8] being instrumental in the building of roads, bridges and churches throughout the O'Conor territories.

Margaret's fame rests, however, not so much on her administrative capabilities as on the two huge feasts she organised to feed the starving. Ireland had long been in a state of tumult, with armies of occupation under both Henry V and VI plundering and ravaging the whole countryside and the principalities constantly at war, in the course of which she and Charles lost their son Con. By 1433 there was widespread famine, which rendered people so emaciated as to be unrecognisable to each other in what became known as 'the summer of slight acquaintance'.[9] In that year, at her personal expense, Margaret caused a gathering of the people to take place at Killeigh, near modern day Tullamore, in County Offaly. The Four Masters record that on this occasion she entertained and feasted the learned men of the land, 2,700 in all. It was not only the artistic coterie and the intelligentsia that she fed, but all who were in need, whatever their station. This chronicle adds that she was herself attired, on these occasions in a magnificent golden robe, sitting above the assembly. Margaret evidently appreciated the value of ceremony when dispensing hospitality. The people were hungry for more than food. In the same year she gave a second hosting, this time at Rathangan, in County Kildare, on the Feast of the Assumption, 15 August, to entertain and provide sustenance for all those who had missed the first. It became as famous as the previous one and affirmed

8 'The Annals of Ireland from the Year 1443 to 1468, Translated from the Irish by Duald MacFirbis', ed. J. O. Donovan, in *Miscellany of the Irish Archeological Society I* (Dublin, 1846), p. 236.
9 E. M. Crawford (ed.), *Famine: The Irish Experience 900–1900* (1989).

Margaret's reputation as a champion of the arts and carer for humanity, earning her the title of Margaret the Hospitable.

Margaret was a fervent Christian as well as a woman of compassion, power and authority. In 1445, when she was no longer young, she set off on a pilgrimage to Compostela in northern Spain, where the bones of St James the Apostle have long been believed to rest in the sanctuary of the Cathedral of Santiago. Pilgrims had streamed to this sacred destination from all over Europe since early times, and there were recognised routes, with hostelries and wayside churches, converging from several directions to the south and west, and with a route from La Coruña for those from the north. It would have been no easy journey, even for a young person: first there was the Bay of Biscay to be crossed in a crowded and insanitary sailing ship; then, even after arriving at La Coruña, there was still a trek of about fifty kilometres to be undertaken, probably on foot. Margaret's joy at first beholding the Romanesque towers can be imagined. She would have obtained entry through a special pilgrims' door and have edged past the gleaming reliquary, embossed in silver, that the modern pilgrim sees today, though not in the sumptuous Baroque setting that was later to add grandeur to the scene. Medieval eyes would have found the reliquary itself, in its holiest of sites beneath the high altar, more than enough of a feast for the eyes and the spirit. The Buddhists have a saying: 'The path is the pilgrim and the pilgrim is the path.' Margaret had made the journey to the spirit that dwelt within her.

She returned home safely, no doubt comforted by the 'Indulgencies' of St James, which assured the recipient's safe entrance into the Kingdom of Heaven through the forgiveness of sins. When she died six years later, in 1451, from breast cancer, Margaret would have considered the loss of her earthly life a fair exchange for the spiritual gift she had received at Compostela, and presumably the scallop shell, the emblem of St James, that all pilgrims cherished as a memento of their holy journey, was buried with her, as was the universal custom. I hope that she, who would have approached the saint's silver coffin at the cathedral of Santiago on her bare knees, was herself enshrouded in the glory of her golden gown.[10]

Bibiana O'Carroll was the wife of Margaret's eldest brother, Mulrony, known as the Bearded. He became Prince of Ely after the death of

10 For almost all the factual content of my account of Margaret O'Carroll I am deeply indebted to Elizabeth Fitzpatrick, then of the Carroll Institute. for her permission to make full use of her essay entitled 'Mairgraig an Einigh O Cearbhaill', written in 1991.

their father. Little is known of Bibiana, but she is famed for having re-endowed the Franciscan monastery at Roscrea, an act of great munificence, and she and her husband are buried there.

Margaret's seventh and youngest child, Finola, was the third female relative of the O'Carrolls of Leap to achieve fame. The Four Masters relate that 'Except for her mother alone, in personal figure and form, in fame and nobility, she was the most distinguished woman in Ireland', and that she went to County Donegal in 1433, with her brother-in-law, to dissuade the O'Neills from making war on her O'Donnell husband. On the death of O'Donnell she married Hugh, the chief of the O'Neills. Obviously she had made a good impression in her ambassadorial role. Finola died in 1493. It is interesting that her lovely name was given, years later, to one of the heroines of this tale, Finola O'Carroll of Leap Castle, said to have married the first Darby to live there.

A clear picture emerges of authority and initiative being displayed by noblewomen of the times. This casts a surprising light on the family structure, which one would have expected to be male-dominated. Margaret the Hospitable is the supreme example of what a woman in those circumstances could achieve and contribute. Seán Ryan has composed a piece of music for her which he plays on his tin whistle, often in the castle, now his home.

The first Prince of Ely thought to have lived at Leap Castle was called John. It is possible that he was responsible for the building of the earliest part of it, and he supposedly died there in 1489,[11] of the plague. John was succeeded by his son, Mulrony O'Carroll, known as the Great Mulrony, and described by the Four Masters as

> the most distinguished man of his time for renown, valour, prosperity and excellence, to whom poets, travellers, ecclesiastics and literary men were most thankful; and who gave most entertainment and bestowed more presents than any other of his lineage...the supporting mainstay of all persons; the rightful, victorious rudder of his race; the powerful young warrior in the march of tribes; the active, triumphant champion of Munster.

11 *The Journal of the Eile Historical Society*, no. 2 1983–1984. Here the date of his death is given as 1447.

A man with such attributes must have had considerable physical presence, while his clothes would have been both stylish and becoming[12] His clansmen must have counted themselves fortunate to have such a leader in what were becoming increasingly dangerous and uncertain times for the O'Carrolls.

By the beginning of the sixteenth century, the boundaries of Ely extended at one point deep into Butler lands, causing unease to the Crown, to whom the Butlers were committed. It had become the habit of England to allow the local Anglo-Irish nobility, the Earls of Ormond (the Butler family) and the Earls of Kildare (the Fitzgeralds), to administer this area of the Midlands, usually with one or the other of those two acting as Lord Deputy. This meant that the O'Carrolls were saddled with the double anxiety of threats from their native Irish neighbours augmented by the menace of England's representatives, themselves landowners, lurking on their borders with an eye to occupation. Survival was becoming more of an issue than aggrandisement; defence more vital than cattle rustling or land grabbing.

In the Great Mulrony's time at Leap, in 1513, the eighth Earl of Kildare, Lord Deputy at the time and anxious to annexe the territory of Ely O'Carroll for England, tried and failed to capture the castle. He was killed by a marksman's arrow shortly afterwards while watering his horse on his way back there with fresh troops. In 1516 his son, the ninth Earl, returned with a formidable force, and after a seven-day siege succeeded in taking Leap, inflicting some structural damage. The O'Carrolls retrieved their castle, having borrowed cannon from Piers Butler, now Earl of Ormond, Mulrony's cousin, with whom he was on good terms. Leap was more than adequately fortified to keep intruders out. The Four Masters remark that 'It is doubtful if there was at that time a castle better fortified and defended.'[13]

During the ensuing years England's intervention in the perpetual disputes between neighbouring powers and her constant attempts to increase her own authority continued to provoke tension in the Midlands. Thomas Howard, Earl of Surrey, had been appointed the new Lord Deputy in 1520. Mulrony must have been an astute diplomat as well as a competent man of action, for it is not long before Surrey refers to him as 'the most esteemed captain in the land'.[14]

12 See Appendix 1.
13 *AFM*, vol. 4, pp. 971–92.
14 *Letters & Papers of Henry VIII*, p. 339.

Now the power structure shifted yet again. Mulrony O'Carroll and Kildare, so recently at loggerheads, became allies, unified in their determination to thwart the ambitions of their overlord, Surrey. This must have infuriated the Englishman, and a nice reflection on the chief's character is seen in his response to Surrey's inviting him to implicate Kildare in an alleged plot to incite rebellion. Mulrony is reported to have smiled and said that 'he would not distain his honour for a pavilion full of gold'. Two of his brothers, similarly interrogated, claimed to be unable to read the seal on a supposedly incriminating letter of Kildare's because they were illiterate.[15]

In 1532 the Great Mulrony died, probably at Leap, after ruling Ely O'Carroll for forty-two years. His fame became legendary and led to a profusion of descendents, direct and otherwise, bearing his illustrious name. This is a trap for chroniclers and confusing for readers. By chance, a similar situation arises later in this book, when most of the Darby heirs are called Jonathan.

Mulrony was succeeded, after a dispute, by his natural son, Fearganhainm, 'The Man without a Name'. It is possible that Mulrony's legitimate son, also named Mulrony, would have got the inheritance had it not been for Fearganainm's recent marriage to the daughter of the ninth Earl of Kildare, now back in the English fold as the Lord Deputy, who intervened on his son-in-law's behalf.

In 1535 Fearganainm, influenced perhaps by a sense of obligation to his wife's family, unwisely involved himself with his Fitzgerald brother-in-law, Lord Offaly, 'Silken Thomas',[16] in the famous Kildare rebellion against the Crown. The uprising failed and resulted in Offaly's execution three years later and the fall from grace of the Kildares. Without a powerful ally, Fearganaimn was swiftly deposed in 1536 by his uncle, Donough O'Carroll, who had allied himself with the Butlers. When Donough died in 1538, Fearganaimn, who had prudently thrown in his lot with Lord Grey, the new Lord Deputy, was reinstated, but at the cost of submission to the Crown, with some fairly crippling obligations thereto. It was at this point that Henry VIII deprived the chief of his title, 'Fearganainm Chief of his Nation', substituting the colourless one of 'Captain of Ely'.[17] I do not suppose any of the locals took much notice of the demotion – this chief was probably a man with two hats.

15 Ibid.
16 So named on account of his fine clothes.
17 *Calender of the Carew Manuscripts 1515–1574*, edd. J. S . Brewer and W. Bullen, vol. 1 (London, 1867), p.141.

He needed to survive at all costs, and to adjust his alliances according to the situation at any given moment.

Fearganainm has been accused by the Four Masters, rightly or wrongly, of the fearful crime of murdering a guest at table, while his steward killed the servant in the guardroom. In another version, the death toll extends to a whole tableful of feasting noblemen and a guardroom packed with revelling attendants. One takes one's choice of horrors. Could there have been extenuating circumstances? Not in the folk tale that this episode became: people like their horrors undiluted.

In 1541 the now old and blind chief was set upon and slain at Clonlisk Castle, another O'Carroll stronghold, together with a dozen of his attendants, by local enemies, the O'Mulloys. The Four Masters comment that for a man of his age he put up a brave resistance.[18] After a dispute, resolved by government intervention, two new chiefs were appointed to rule jointly, Fearganaimn's son Thady, known as 'The One-Eyed', and his cousin Charles. Thady quickly took command.

Since the Kildares were still out of favour, the new chief judged that the main threat to his power, more alarming even than that from the Butlers, now lay with the English. In 1541 Henry VIII took the title of King of Ireland, and in the following year Thady visited him to seek the status of tenant-in-chief, which would give him equality under the Crown with both the Kildares and the Butlers. This would have been quite an undertaking for an Irish chief, with journeys by land, sea, and then more land, to an unfamiliar destination, and there could have been no certain outcome from an audience with that wayward and unpredictable monarch. However, the king was exceedingly gracious and gave Thady twenty pounds.[19] Two years later this chief managed to get back some of the O'Carroll lands that the Butlers had appropriated, setting fire to Nenagh, their garrison town.[20]

In 1552, during Edward VI's short reign, One-Eyed Thady's opportunistic loyalty to the Crown was recognised by the Lord Deputy with a knighthood. He was subsequently given the title of Lord Baron of Ely, an honour he was to enjoy for only a few months, since his cousin Charles, whom he had utterly dominated as co-ruler, assassinated him in 1553,[21] to become the chief. Charles in turn was murdered by his

18 *AFM*, vol. 5, p. 417.
19 *Letters & Papers of Henry VIII, 1542*, pp. 460, 480.
20 M. Archdall, *Monasticum Hibernicum* (1786), p. 672.
21 *AFM*, vol. 5, p. 444.

brother, William Odhar, 'The Pale' or 'Dull', who ruled Ely from 1554 for many years.

We have to appreciate the anxiety and apprehension which must have dominated the life of an O'Carroll Prince. He needed to have eyes in the back of his head to remain aware of all the changes of allegiance and policy which went on around him, endangering other principalities as well as his own, as England gradually tightened her grip. Moreover, there was constant rivalry for the title of chief among his own family, which seems to have been stronger, on occasion, than brotherly love. Survival was all, even if that entailed a degree of subjugation to the Crown, which might not be permanent. To a warlike people such as the O'Carrolls, death would not have been held in too much account: in a tight corner, with your own future and that of your principality hanging in the balance, you either killed or got killed.

It was during William the Pale's chieftaincy at Leap, just before Queen Mary Tudor was succeeded by Elizabeth, that the castle was for the first time attacked by an English force. It was led by Henry Radcliffe, Earl of Sussex, the new Lord Deputy, in pursuance of his aim to enforce the colonisation, or 'plantation', plans for the area.[22] In *The Carew Manuscripts* there is the following record of the affair:

> On Tuesday, 14th. June 1558, my Lord Deputy camped a little above the Island of Kelle Tobber in O'Carroll's country. Lenny Banny [Leap Castle] was set on fire before we came to it, and the castle broken. They of the ward of the castle of Kelle Tobber shot at our men.... William Cautenell, my Lord's interpreter, was sent to them once or twice on a message.[23]

A different account is given by the Four Masters. They maintain that Sussex, in pursuit of the O'Conors, kinsmen of the O'Carrolls who had taken refuge at Leap, actually took the castle. They add that the chief got away. 'It was the goodness of his steed', say the Masters, that saved him.[24] They go on to report that the castle was recaptured shortly afterwards by William, who 'found it undefended'. It is upon this occasion that the Darby family believed that a Darby-O'Carroll romantic alliance, described in chapter 4, took place, regardless, it seems, of any but the remotest possibility.

22 See p. 40.
23 *Calender of the Carew Manuscripts 1557–1574* (London, 1867), p. 274.
24 *AFM*, vol. 5, p. 1547.

William the Pale continued to have trouble with the English during his early days as chief. The forces of the Crown were not sufficiently numerous to overrun Ely O'Carroll and claim it, but Sussex tried to impose his authority by deposing William for alleged treachery in 1558, in favour of a relative named Thady. Once Sussex's back was turned he quickly reinstated himself, driving this Thady out in January 1559.[25] Thereafter attempts were made by the Queen's representatives to achieve cooperation with this powerful chief rather than meet him head-on in conflict. He seems to have been a stout-hearted leader, in spite of his anaemic appearance.

The Butlers, on the other hand, remained hostile and rapacious. There are numerous instances on record of their attacks upon the O'Carrolls and their territories around this time. In 1568 William's wife, Sabina (or Savery) FitzPatrick, the mother of some but not all of her husband's sons, writes to the Lord Deputy, in Latin, as follows:

> We have just discovered that you wanted myself and Thaddeus and Donald and certain others to visit your place to reply to Edward Butler's complaints against my case. My reply to this is that I have twice visited your place to put forward my complaints against Edward and to reply to him respectfully with regard to all his complaints. But he, without giving any notice, stubbornly kept away and made extra expense for me. So I am all the more certain that he will stay away in just the same manner. Therefore if your Honour really wishes to summon Edward before you on a fixed date and at a fixed place, I am concerned both whether I would see Edward respecting your laws and attending without any delay on the correct date of the meeting, when I and the O'Carroll sons would be with you, and that it would be troublesome for me? In the third place there's the expense, and since Edward has a large army positioned on the boundaries of my estate and I am uncertain whether he wishes to harm myself or my estate, please receive my apologies for the present: may you keep in good health,
> From Leirmhibanan, 3rd September,
> Your humble servant
> Savery ffitzpatrick Lady of Ely.[26]

25 R. Cox, *Hibernia Anglicana* (London, 1962, 2nd edition), pp. 286–7.

26 Carte MSS LVIII F. 671, Bodleian Library, Oxford. Translated from the Latin by Henrietta Freeman-Attwood.

Sabina was obviously a woman of courage, intelligence and authority. Perhaps she even knew Latin and composed this letter herself, sitting in one of the embrasured windows of the keep at Leap. Her husband was away at the time, looking to his territory's safety from his castle at Clonlisk, some six miles away. With the Butlers threatening Ely on all sides, William and his sons were fortunate in having so diplomatic and supportive a Lady of Ely as wife and mother. I think of her as looking rather like Vanessa Redgrave.

The English under Elizabeth continued to be increasingly active in their efforts to bring Ireland under their sway once and for all. In 1567 Sir William had been knighted at Limerick, which placed him under some obligation to the Crown. Eventually, in 1578, perhaps thinking that the English would at last afford him some protection from the Butlers and other predatory neighbours, William Odhar O'Carroll made his submission to Elizabeth,[27] together with thirty-eight freeholders from other parts of Ely. These included William O'Banane (O'Bannon), a descendant of the two brothers whose association with the castle's name is related in chapter 3.

The submission took place under an arrangement known as surrender and regrant. This was a procedure initiated in Henry VIII's time, whereby the English monarch claimed the property in question, after which it would be returned to its previous owner in exchange for an oath of loyalty, regular sums of money, and an undertaking to provide troops for the Crown when required. As Henry, renownedly handy with the pen, had rather engagingly put it in 1520, in a letter to his Lord Deputy:

> We and our Council think, and verily believe, that in case circumspect and politic ways be used, you shall bring the Irish lords to obedience, ...which thing must as yet rather be practised by sober ways, politic drifts, and amiable persuasions ... than by rigorous dealing...[28]

That was not at all the O'Carroll way of doing things. Hawkish, they would not have held with effete methods like amiable persuasion, but the position of William Odhar O'Carroll, always precarious, had become extremely vulnerable, and Elizabeth was herself very keen on incentives. The agreement was advantageous to both parties, gaining

27 The submission document is housed in the Tower of London.
28 *State Papers*, Henry VIII, Ireland.

for the monarchy a loyal (in theory) subject, and the owner the assurance that his firstborn son would succeed him by the law of 'primogeniture' in a now compromised inheritance. Knighthoods were subsequently conferred by Her Majesty on two of Sir William's sons, Charles and Mulrony. Titles were often given to the families of collaborating noblemen to sweeten the pill. How the O'Carrolls must have hated the situation! But perhaps they quite enjoyed having a handle to their name even while affecting to despise such things, and saw this pragmatic arrangement as inevitable.

Sir William lived on to a ripe old age, repelling his ambitious kinsmen, wheeling and dealing with his neighbours when not carrying out raids against them, and in and out of trouble with the English. Never very safely in the saddle, he was set upon and done to death by a party of his O'Conor relations in 1581 who, according to the Four Masters, 'threw his body to the wolves and ravens'. He had ruled for twenty-seven years. Other assassinations followed, for there were many who felt that, despite the law of primogeniture, they had a better right than any other to the chieftaincy.

Sir William was succeeded by his son John, according to the new law, but John was murdered the following year by his cousin Mulrony, son of One-Eyed Thady. John's murder was at once avenged by his illegitimate brother Charles, who, having killed Mulrony, became Prince of Ely as the rightful successor to his father. Despite the carnage Charles was accepted as chief by the English. He was knighted in 1586.

It seems that, as England closed in for the kill, the O'Carrolls persevered in their old way of settling family disputes. It is as if they were hacking their way through a jungle composed not of vegetation but of other human beings. These were among the darkest days of their history (I have reported by no means all of the recorded family murders, often committed in complicated sub-plots), and many of the worst atrocities are believed to have taken place within the walls of Leap. The amount of human bones unearthed there, not to mention those immured, would seem to bear this out, and where there are bones there must have been much blood, fury and pain, sunk into the stone and into the collective memory of the O'Carrolls.

Sir Charles held sway for some time, by the standards of the day, in spite of the ongoing hostility of his neighbours and lack of active support from the English. On one occasion in 1596, evidently driven to exasperation, he writes to Lord Burghley, Elizabeth's Treasurer and Chief Adviser, complaining that in his absence the Earl of Ormond had overrun his territory, attacked his castle and killed several O'Carrolls, including the chief's own nephew and heir, another Mulrony. Moreover, he continues, these marauding Butlers had made off with all his horses and 1,200 head of cattle.[29] Sir Charles got Leap back, badly damaged but not destroyed, and the Butler incursions continued unremittingly, in battle and in the law courts, in spite of the supposedly stabilising influence of the surrender and regrant policy.

For some time after he succeeded to the castle and its lands, Sir Charles, himself a murderer, had been making efforts to safeguard his property from family feuding and from the continual incursions of the Butlers in pursuit of their ancient but unratified title to the O'Carroll lands, which had now been going on for nearly 400 years. In 1589 he petitioned the Privy Council,[30] stating that the only hope of peace and stability in the area lay in the 'shiring' of Ely O'Carroll and some of its neighbours, creating a newly defined territory belonging to the Crown, or in the inclusion of his territory in the already existing King's County.[31] The chief's plea was in vain, for the wily powers that be took a cynical view, reflecting the motivation behind many acts of submission. This is summed up in a letter from Sir Ralph Lane, the then Deputy, to Lord Burghley in 1597, which contains the observation:

> Sir Charles O'Carroll and Sir John McCoghlan both are lords of great countries; both have been rebels and more rebellious minds are not in Ireland; yet both are subjects: but why? They have rivals. There be others have more right to their lands than themselves: if they be not subjects they lose both land and lives. Their surrender to Her Majesty is their only security. These and others are commended for good subjects for their cutting off of the heads of some of their name and nation; but those heads which they send in are better pledges of their own security than any kind of assurance of their loyalties…[32]

Tactics were all-important in maintaining order in Ireland. The queen's advisors, who had been so free with bribes to get the chiefs under her sway, now favoured the policy of keeping all parties weak

29 Sir Charles O'Carroll to the Privy Council, 2 July 1596.*Calender of State Papers.*
30 *Calender of State Papers.*
31 Named by Queen Mary, after her husband King Philip of Spain. The adjacent shire was named Queen's County, after herself.They are now Offaly and Leix respectively.
32 *Calender of State Papers 1596–97.*

and fearful of each other. This was a bitter time for Sir Charles, who remained a loyal servant of Elizabeth, even when Ely O'Carroll was overrun by the famous Hugh O'Neill, the Earl of Tyrone, in the Great Rebellion in 1598, and many O'Carrolls agitated to join the invader against the English. By that time the Chief was losing his authority: the Crown did not intervene. In the same year Sir Charles wrote a desperate letter to Lord Burghley, which lists his sufferings, begs for troops to repel his enemies and ends: 'For I have imbrued my hands so far in traitors' blood as I must violently persecute them, or they will have my life. I never was in more distress, and there for let me be comforted now or never.'[33]

Burghley seems, predictably, to have done nothing to help. Sir Charles lived on, powerless and in misery, until 1600, when he was slain by some 'petty gentlemen of the O'Carrolls and O'Meaghers'[34] in revenge for a terrible crime he committed in the previous year, when he must surely have been unhinged by despair. According to the Four Masters, Sir Charles hired some noblemen of the McMahons of Oriel, together with a hundred of their troops, for some enterprise, when perhaps he was uncertain of the loyalty of his own people. When the time came to pay them, 'O'Carroll and his people went to them by night and slew them in their beds…'.[35]

After Sir Charles's murder, the Tyrone supporters within the clan seized power and Tyrone again invaded Ely O'Carroll, this time setting fire to everything in his path before moving on further into Munster. Four O'Carrolls, including Sir Charles's own brother Mulrony, one of the foremost rebels, competed for leadership, splitting the clan into segments. Sir George Carew duly reported to the Privy Council at the time of Sir Charles's death:

> This last week…Sir Charles O'Carroll, (a good servant of Her Majesty's) was murdered by one of his kinsmen. Four of the O'Carrolls are in competition for the lordship of that country. Before that question is settled it will cost much blood but therein the state is nothing indemnified.[36]

This warning appears to have been heeded by the Privy Council, who intervened in the name of peace and order, insisting that the law of primogeniture be upheld.

33 *Calender of State Papers, 1599.*
34 *Ireland under the Commonwealth* (Manchester, 1913), vol. 1, p. 24.
35 *AFM*, 1599.
36 *Calender of State Papers 1599–1600*, p. 416.

Sir Charles O'Carroll's great-nephew John was the last in line for the title of Chief of Ely. John was a baby when his father Mulrony was put to death by that marauding party of Butlers in 1596, and in 1600 he was officially named as the new chief. In 1605 John was made a ward of court at the behest of James I, who succeeded Elizabeth in 1603. We know that efforts were made to anglicise him, for in 1612 the Lords of the Privy Council announced that John's wardens wished him to be brought up at the College of Dublin (Trinity College) 'or some place of learning in England'.[37] In the meantime, Leap and its territories were governed by several wardens. One of these, Sir Charles's brother Mulrony, the boy's uncle, was pardoned for his part in the Tyrone insurrection and actually knighted on the Coronation Day of James I. Expediency was more powerful than justice where the imposition of order was concerned. In due course, John O'Carroll was recalled, but Ely O'Carroll was already under some degree of plantation, so that the chieftancy was virtually extinct. In 1605 the 'shiring' of the territory, begged for by poor Sir Charles, had finally taken place: it became part of King's County.

In 1629 Charles I, who had come to the throne four years earlier, gave his official approval of John's possession of Leap and its surrounding land because he had accepted the plantation plans, yielding up much of his estate. He would have had no choice. A number of other noble O'Carrolls remained in possession of at least some of their property. John's background doubtless inclined him towards loyalty to the Crown, to which both his father Charles and his grandfather William had been, by and large, faithful. The brainwashing to which the youth had been subjected clearly paid off too, for at the time of the Catholic revolt of 1641[38] he remained faithful to his king, although many of the O'Carroll clan took part. His was no 'rebellious mind': at long last here was an O'Carroll who could be relied upon to hunt with the hounds without running with the hare. He is twice described as Receiver of Enemy Estates in the King's County in 1647 in the *Calender of State Papers*[39] when so-called justice was being meted out to rebellious noblemen, but it did him no good in the long run – he lost his lands like everyone else in the district.

37 Ibid. *1611–1614*, p. 279.

38 This began in Ulster, starting a chain of events. Presbyterian Scots took up arms in self-defence and the insurgence spread throughout the land, continuing sporadically until Cromwell's ruthless campaign in Ireland in 1649, after the defeat and beheading of Charles, which crushed the rebellion.

39 *1633–1647*, pp. 733 & 744.

So ends my outline history of the O'Carrolls of Ely. Heroic deeds, shrewd diplomacy, liberal munificence and patronage of the arts intersperse with horrifying chains of family murders as the once great dynasty moved inexorably towards the enforced termination of its ancient rule. It is odd that the killings reached a climax so comparatively late in the history of the area, when some stabilising structures were already in place. It seems that each of the senior O'Carroll noblemen was out for himself at a time when the Crown was gradually getting a stranglehold on the old despotic regimes and imposing its own none too subtle domination.

John Dymock, who compiled his *Treatise on Ireland* in the late sixteenth century, writing about the explosive situation in Ely, concludes his piece as follows: 'It hath small piles of little importance, the chiefest whereof is Limwaddon [Leap].' Small piles of little importance! These strongholds, built with the sweat of O'Carroll brows, defended with their hearts' blood, became the bastions of a beleaguered kingdom. They fell in the end to foreign forces of overwhelming strength who then installed one of the ancient clan as the puppet landlord of a fragment of Ely O'Carroll lands, with the empty title of John Carroll of The Leape.[40]

I often think about John Carroll. Did he lose his mother as well as his father? Events had made her a pawn of fortune, like her little son, and we cannot know if she was able or indeed inclined to hang onto him, at least until he was sent away to be made into a yes-man.

PART TWO: THE PLANTATION, AND AFTER

In order to give a clear picture of the sequence of events that led up to the end of all O'Carroll influence in Ely, and to the confiscation of all their lands, I must go back to 1620. In that year, under James I, Ely O'Carroll was officially 'planted'. Plantation was a form of colonisation designed to be specifically applicable to Ireland. It consisted of peopling an area with English or Scottish Protestant families known as 'undertakers', who were prepared to occupy land hitherto belonging to the Irish, to farm it productively and, over a period of time, to import other Protestants to squeeze out many of the native population and, in doing so, to establish a pronounced local Protestant majority. This had worked well in Ulster when the king introduced it there in 1603 and, it

40 The prefix 'O' was by now disallowed.

was assumed, would present the solution to the unstable condition of the Irish Midlands, in the centre of which lay the kingdom of Ely O'Carroll. What better place to introduce plantation? The area was already in the hands of the Crown, and since Sir Charles Carroll had remained more or less loyal throughout his sad and difficult tenure, there would be no question of penalising his descendants unduly. John Carroll of The Leape and other landed members of his clan would, in theory, remain in possession of two-thirds of their native soil. All this hung fire, mainly for lack of money, and because of the general unrest and the habitual unruliness of the inhabitants, who naturally objected to the reduction of their territory in furtherance of the colonists' aim.

There might well have been a total stalemate, but for the arrival on the scene of Laurence Parsons. He was the younger brother of Sir William Parsons, Surveyor General in Ireland. Sir William, who had already given Laurence the job of Clerk of the Peace in Munster, saw him appointed, in 1620, as Receiver General and patentee of all Crown lands in Ireland. Birr Castle was to be the Englishman's headquarters. Gradually, under Laurence Parsons's authority, the tide began to turn decisively in favour of the settlers, with the Receiver General not unnaturally feathering his own nest and enabling others to do the same.

Sir Laurence, as he soon became, set about establishing himself as a landowner at a most advantageous time, but in 1641 rebellion broke out in Ulster. This, as every Irishman knows, was led by the Catholic landowners following the recall and execution for treason of the Earl of Strafford, the Lord Deputy. The whole country was soon in a state of chaos, with the English army temporarily driven out of Ely O'Carroll.

Also in 1641, Sir Laurence died and his son, Captain William Parsons, was made Governor of Birr Castle and granted permission to garrison it. Meanwhile, in accordance with agreed English policy, all but the most recalcitrant of the noble Carrolls, twenty-three of them in all, retained their homes and some of their land, with 15,906 acres between them.[41] The English 'adventurers', as the new influx of colonists were called, took advantage of the turbulent state of the area and continued to grab whatever land they could lay their hands on.

The year 1649 was a black and bloody one for Ireland. After the execution of Charles I and the establishment of the Commonwealth, Oliver Cromwell and his army of Roundheads arrived to crush the rebellion. Ruthlessly, they laid waste to huge areas and committed wholesale

41 *The Down Survey* (1654–9), compiled by Sir William Petty.

atrocities during their leader's campaign to subdue the country permanently. The Civil War in England had used up all Cromwell's resources and he gave his soldiers Irish property and land in lieu of pay. A contingent of his troops (not the hideously misnamed Lord Protector himself, as my family predictably claimed) arrived at Leap, where John Carroll and his retinue lived, and threatened, say the Four Masters, to 'blow them out with a pumpstick' if the occupants resisted. Leap, as we have seen, could not withstand cannon shot, and was especially vulnerable from the high ground nearby. The assumption is that the attackers met with no resistance.

Although there is much confusion over the matter, it is likely that at this time or a little later the first Darby, probably an officer in the Commonwealth force that had taken the castle, became the owner of Leap. This is borne out by the Poll Tax account of 1659 which contains the entry, 'Leape, Jonathen Derby gent. (tituladoe) 4 English, 17 Irish'.

In 1660, at the start of the Restoration, Charles II, in a cleft stick, upheld the Cromwellian conquest while undertaking to restore to 'innocent Papists' some of their property. What of Leap? Jonathan Darby must have felt distinctly insecure in his new abode, especially when in 1664 nominees for restitution of their homes and lands presented their names to the now unassailable and socially upgraded head of the Butler family, the Duke of Ormond, Governor of Ireland. Ormond selected a number of these and restored to them minimal amounts of their previous lands, some regaining only their dwellings and parks. There were nine Carroll applicants, with nine castles, most of whom had to be content with less than 100 acres of surrounding land, though John Carroll of the Leape got 200 and his namesake of Clonlisk 500 acres on the grounds that, unlike some of their less consistent family and neighbours, they had remained loyal to Charles I and subsequently were among those who 'manifested their good affections to His Majesty's service'.[42] As a result of this verdict John Carroll, or his brother (around this time they seem to have exchanged castles), was reinstated. Jonathan Darby and such of his family and retainers as were by then in residence must have had to move out, having scarcely had time to find their feet in their new home.

It is difficult to imagine how this fluctuating situation would have affected the protagonists. Did the Carrolls and Darbys, in these shifting conditions, hand the keys back and forth to each other in the castle

42 From the list of principal dispossessed landowners presented to the Duke of Ormond in 1664.

doorway, haggling the while over the livestock and furnishings? Where did the Darbys go? A fearful sense of insecurity and uncertainty must have pervaded the castle, reflecting the whole state of Ireland itself.

By 1667 Charles II's government had evidently gone back on the previous arrangement whereby John Carroll had had his property restored to him. It seems that by that date the castle was once more in the hands of one 'Jonathan Darby of Leape',[43] and thereafter that family held the estate in perpetuity. However, it must be said that establishing ownership of the castle and land at this time is complicated by the shadowy presence of a John Holland to whom Jonathan Darby was said variously to have sold or mortgaged them.[44] This is a grey area, complicated by the Darby family's assertion that they had been installed at Leap many years previously, but not one of much importance to this story except insofar as it illustrates the general state of confusion.

Throughout the seventeenth century all the Carrolls (as we must now call them, by government decree) who had been given back their homes would probably have lost and regained them several times over, but the vast majority of them supported Catholic James II (Charles II's brother) against his son-in-law William of Orange during the Battle of the Boyne in 1689. After the Treaty of Limerick in 1691,[45] when the Protestant William had finally defeated James and become king, they lost their estates irretrievably and the remainder of the O'Carroll lands passed into the hands of the Parsons, Darby and Lloyd families. Most of the young Carrolls, like other uprooted Catholic swordsmen, some 3,400 in all, packed up what they could salvage of their belongings and enlisted in Irish brigades in foreign armies, leaving their homeland for ever. These young men were known as 'wild geese'.[46]

The Carroll wild geese were the first of a stream of Carrolls who emigrated to avoid persecution by the English and later to escape terrible famine. Many others went to America, and one of these, Charles Carroll of the Ely clan, settled with his family in Maryland, in 1688, at a

43 See Burke's *Irish Family Records*.

44 The suggestion of a mortgage on the estate is based, at least partly, on the myth of the royalist Wild Captain, whose defiance of Parliament reputedly made his son, Jonathan, apprehensive of his land being confiscated after Charles I was defeated in the Civil War. To avoid confiscation by Parliament because of his father's record, this Jonathan is supposed to have mortgaged his land to John Holland. A different version of this tale is related in Cooke's *History of Birr*. I can find no documentary verification for either story.

45 In exchange for the surrender of their last stronghold in Limerick, Jacobite soldiers were offered free passage to France.

46 See Appendix 2.

place they named Carrolton. His grandson, also Charles Carroll,[47] distinguished himself in public affairs and commerce and was a signatory of the American Declaration of Independence in 1776, the only Catholic to be so. In the words of Alistair Cooke: '... he outlived all the other signers and died, at the age of ninety-five, the richest man in America.'[48] The *Dictionary of American Biography* lists four other Carrolls, including the Most Reverend John Carroll,[49] the first Catholic bishop in the United States, but they may not all have been descendants of the O'Carrolls of Ely.

No one is alive today who has any inkling of what documents were held in the castle archives in a supposedly fire-proof safe.[50] Had those archives survived they might have shed light on exactly what did happen to Leap after its capture in Cromwell's time; family information that would not have got into the public records. There might even have been clues about the alleged intermarriage of a Darby with an O'Carroll, either then or earlier, about which we can only speculate. My grandmother states in a letter to her friend Sydney Carroll just after the fire that 'ALL land and estate papers [are] gone between the Record etc. in the Four Courts[51] and now our own copies....'

It is heartbreaking to dwell on what may have been lost, but there is consolation in the fact that, within recent years, an enormous amount of hitherto unpublished information about the whole area has been revealed by modern scholarship, and more is coming to light all the time.

47 1737–1832.
48 Alistair Cooke's *America,* BBC Publications 1973, p. 121.
49 1735–1815.
50 All that survives is the badly scorched Final Concord of 1641 and two transcripts of fines in the reigns of William and Mary and of Queen Anne.
51 The seat of the Supreme Court and Public Record Office in Dublin, badly damaged by shellfire four weeks before Leap was burned down.

3
The Castle: Architectural History and Hearsay

In the previous chapter the confusing, heroic and bloody struggles of the O'Carrolls of Ely to survive individually and as a nation came to an ignominious end, with them playing Box and Cox with the English interlopers in their main fortress, Leap Castle.

What was the castle like, and how did it evolve? There is still much to be discovered about its origins, but the following account will give some idea of what one family lost and another gained.

Leap stands on a 635 feet high ridge, under the hill of Knock, in the barony of Ballybritt in the heart of the Irish Midlands. It is a mere forty miles south of the Rock of Divisions, or *umbilicus Hiberniae,* regarded as the very centre of Ireland.[1] As one of the chief strongholds of the O'Carrolls of Ely during their last century and a half of power, it is marked on all the important maps of the sixteenth and seventeenth centuries. There are various theories as to how it got its name; suffice it to say that it was originally called *Leim-ui-Banain*, O'Bannon's Leap in English, in reference to the O'Bannons, already mentioned as one of the O'Carroll subject clans who ruled over the area known as *Hy Dechi*, in which Leap Castle stood. This part of Ely is described by the fifteenth-century poet O'Heedrin as 'the extensive land of fair fortresses'.

The most commonly quoted version of the legend is that two O'Bannon brothers, both claimants to the castle and its lands, leaped together from a crag, having agreed that the survivor should inherit. Luckily, one did. The castle later became known as Lemyvane, a corruption of the above, and also as Lemyvadon, which name appears on the map of the area in *Mercator's Atlas* in 1623. The English spelt the name in a variety of ways, true to their tendency to substitute their own version of any foreign word with which they have difficulty. When it later became known simply as The Leap, other notions as to the origin

1 Giraldus Cambrensis, twelfth-century chronicler.

of the name proliferated.[2] That they could not all be true troubled no one; romantic associations clung like ivy to the grim walls, making them seem less bare, less detached from the cauldron of human emotions that bubbled away inside for most of Leap's life.

The castle was strategically placed to guard the Fuarawn river to the east and the pass through the Slieve Bloom mountains leading south into Tipperary, and its territory was further protected by an arc of little fortresses, some of which still survive. It was thought in Victorian times to have existed in some form before the Danish invasions and subsequently to have been rebuilt by the Danes and wrested from them by the Irish in about AD 900. Some evidence was supposed to point to the castle having been partly reconstructed after the Anglo-Norman invasions in 1169 in Henry II's time. None of this was ever questioned by any of my forebears of recent times, whose own notions corresponded with those professed by the experts. Historians up until comparatively modern days did not believe that the Irish themselves were capable of castle building, even in its earliest form, and proclaimed that they learnt these skills from the Normans, but modern research disputes this.

In view of the O'Carroll clan history it is probable that there was some earlier building of the same name on or near the site of the present castle, but the central portion of Leap is now reckoned to be a 'tower house' of the early sixteenth century.[3] Tower houses were built in considerable numbers from the mid-fourteenth century onwards, replacing the wooden structures hitherto occupied by the lesser nobility. As their name implies, they were plain towers standing foursquare, sometimes, as in in Leap's case, slightly broader at the base. They were constructed as fortified residences, less massive than the earlier strongholds which had had to withstand large-scale invasion from foreign troops. However, the O'Carrolls took no chances regarding possible incursions from neighbouring septs or contingents of English forces on the make. The walls of Leap are very stout, in places over four metres thick. Secret corridors and at least three spiral staircases threaded their way through the middle of these walls, one leading to a machicolation which still juts out from the south side of the keep where the original entrance was. A machicolation is an overhanging stone balcony with a sluice in its floor

2 The Ordnance Survey letters of 1838 state, unconvincingly, that the name referred to some local feature, prior to the erection of the castle. Mr George Cunningham favours derivation from the Irish word '*Leim*', an animal track.

3 *Archeological Inventory of Offaly* (1997), p. 150.

through which boiling pitch could be poured onto invaders, while rocks hurled over the edge would be a further deterrent. There may have been more of these machicolations at one time. There were also murder holes, situated above doorways and at strategic points round the castle, whence you could fire arrows or drop boulders onto anyone who had penetrated the outer defences. One of these narrow conduits between the inner and outer parts of the wall led to the lavatory, called the 'guardrobe' because ammonia fumes which issued from the depths were utilised to delouse the inhabitants' garments, which could be hung within range of the stench. The term 'cloakroom' has survived, interestingly, on account of its supposed delicacy compared with the word lavatory.

Leap was a fine example of its kind. It was built of limestone rubble, hammer dressed inside, with chiselled stones at the corners and around windows and doorways. Sometimes these were ornamented – a sign of the more relaxed, less hostile spirit in which tower houses were built. This castle has some elegant, slightly ogee-arched windows in the upper chamber, known in recent times as the Bloody Chapel. The first floor would have been made of heavy oak planks covered with rushes or straw. There was, however, often a vault of stone supporting an upper level. Leap had one such beneath the floor of its upper room. These vaults were held in position during construction by arches comprised of wickerwork mats on temporary timber trusses. The high-pitched roof would be made of timber covered with stone, slates or thatch. It seems unlikely that so imposing a residence as Leap would have been thatched, as some lesser castles were, particularly since such a roof was vulnerable to firing from flaming arrows, but the gabled ends, rising from the inside of the square outer walls, give us no clue about that. It is probable that the whole edifice was limewashed, standing out palely against the bog, forest and pasture that surrounded it, like a castle in a medieval illuminated Book of Hours. A 'fair fortress' to be sure. Leap is reputed to have originally sported a carved *Seila na Gig*, an obscene female grotesque, on the south wall of the keep. These were commonly found on Irish castles and were supposed to deter raiders. I wonder who took it down?

The castle would have been very dark inside, even with limewashed walls to reflect what light did penetrate its windows, which are wide-arched inside, narrowing towards the exterior. It would have been cold too, in spite of tapestries hung in particularly draughty areas, like the arras at the castle of Elsinore behind which old Polonius so unwisely lurked to eavesdrop in *Hamlet*. There were also two huge fireplaces, still there but until recently hanging in a chasm, Magritte-like, together with old iron bedsteads that teetered on stone corbels where floors had fallen in during the burning. There is still one of these, propped up in the garden. Who slept on it? Could my mother have dreamed of my father, pillowed against its bars?

Tower houses such as Leap were surrounded by a walled courtyard, or bawn, with corner turrets and a machicolated gateway and at Leap there was also a moat. A secret tunnel ran westwards for some 100 yards to a former rath, or fortification, and was used to get supplies, including live animals, into the castle during sieges. My grandfather claimed to know its whereabouts, but never disclosed this information to anyone. The story goes that a cow once fell through the roof of the tunnel and wandered, mooing, in the basement, for several days before anyone was brave enough to confront what was thought to be a particularly terrifying ghoul.

There was often a single-storied building for domestic purposes, close by the tower, where food and drink was served on low tables, with couches to recline on such as the Romans had. There is reason to suppose that Leap had such a hall, possibly behind where the additional building known as the Priest's House now stands, for this was a family home, not just a fortress, and would have had its complement of old people, women and children as well as warriors. The whole place must have reverberated with many of the noises you may still hear in large family houses – shouts, complaints and laughter, the clanging of cooking utensils, the barking of dogs and, from time to time, music, played and sung in those days by travelling musicians or by the inhabitants themselves. On top of that, horsemen and wheeled vehicles would have been continually clattering in and out of the compound. All this was the norm; but there were times of peril when the non-combatant inmates cowering in the basements would hear the cries of some unfortunate victim either riven by a sword or battleaxe, clubbed or, worse still, scalded by boiling pitch. History does not relate whether or not the enemy wounded were tended when the battle was over. It seems unlikely that they would be given the chance to fight another day. A horrible-looking blackthorn club, or '*shellelagh*', much prized by my grandfather, still survives, and was said by him to have bludgeoned many an O'Carroll foe into the next world. It was highly polished and served as a macabre ornament in our house when I was small.

The building known as the Priest's House was built not long after the tower house itself, as can be seen both from its foundations and from a print of Leap made in the eighteenth century, in which it retains its late medieval and early Tudor character. It stood on its own, two stories high, with cellars for storage and a chimney stack, and there is a much-battered chimneypiece still standing. An oak beam within this was recently dated by dendrochronology[4] and is said to be of around 1571. Some delicate window-sills are likely to belong to the late seventeenth century. The Priest's House was clearly some sort of dwelling in peaceful times, but no one has yet discovered how it came by that name. One explanation is that there may have been a priest in residence who attended to the spiritual needs of the village surrounding the castle as well as to outlying settlements belonging to it. There are several priest's houses attached to English manor houses; at Sissinghurst Castle, for instance, there is one within the grounds although the chapel has gone. There could have been a chapel adjacent to the Priest's House at Leap. If so, when the Protestant Darbys and their employees arrived, the services of the priest would have been peremptorily dispensed with and the dwelling put to another use. It was certainly updated from time to time thereafter. Priest's houses in England were the Catholic forerunners of the parsonages that sprang up after the Reformation.The Darbys themselves, however, always maintained that the Priest's House was originally where the O'Carrolls lived in peacetime, and that they all moved into the main tower only when the castle was under attack. If this is true, why did it acquire its distinctive name? Probably because of its resident ghost, a monk or perhaps a priest, of whom more will be heard later. Nothing at Leap proclaims its function without embellishment; even the telegraph poles skirting the property are swathed in thick ivy, its tendrils entwining themselves along the wire, as if bent on penetrating the friendly talk of neighbours with dark insinuations.

The ground floor, or great hall, of the castle had another large room on top of it, barrel vaulted and with a handsome fireplace – the one recently opened up by Seán Ryan. The second storey surmounting this room gives access to exterior walkways, from which the castle could be defended and bodies thrown. It was in a corner of this top room, the bloody chapel, that the infamous 'oubliette', was situated, concealed by

4 This consists of counting the rings of the tree from which the beam was constructed by means of a cross-section of the beam. Alison Rosse instigated this invaluable investigation.

a trapdoor in the floor, probably hidden under rushes. Victims would be lured into position and then the trap would be sprung by a secret mechanism, dropping them, avowedly via a series of revolving knives operated by a ratchet, onto a spike in a dungeon hewn out of the rock below the level of the castle's foundations. The ratchet is probably a gruesome folkloric embellishment, but in Hieronymus Bosch's[5] depiction of Hell in his famous picture, *The Garden of Pleasant Delights,* there is a demon operating a ratchet, with a tower behind it that is terrifyingly reminiscent of Leap to one brought up on the ratchet story. Oubliettes were common in Irish castles and that this one was used well into the eighteenth century is suggested by the watch parts said to have been discovered among the bones when the oubliette was investigated before being partially filled in in my grandparents' day.[6] I am doubtful about this suspiciously neat detail, with its double reference to the passing of time. What became of these relics, if they ever existed? Hearsay seems so often to masquerade as veracity where Leap is concerned that the chronicler is torn between trust and scepticism and craves for a fact.

The presence of the oubliette within the confines of a consecrated place seems unlikely, which reinforces my supposition that this upper chamber was not at first used as a chapel at all. Some authorities think it was originally the banqueting hall, at a level deemed safe from assault, where revellers could pass out in safety and snore the night away as the candles guttered out.

At one time the top room at Leap had been given a stone roof. It fell in and was replaced in the nineteenth century. By now there were numerous walled-in chambers, staircases and passages, taking up about a third of the whole castle, though who filled them in, and why, no one can say. The blocked up areas within the house must have been unsettling to the sensitive, particularly as in some cases their glazed windows still pierced the exterior, redolent of secrecy, capable only of random reflection. Thumps and bumps were sometimes heard in these shut-off places, my grandmother said, probably caused by rats or large birds that had found a way in, but felt by her to be more mysterious, more sinister.

On the south east corner, a guardroom is hewn out of the rock face. This was unearthed in my great-great-grandfather's time, about 1870. Grandfather himself, when he inherited from his grandfather in 1880,

5 He died in 1516.

6 My aunt Cecily wrote, in a letter to a newspaper: 'My father filled it in to the present level.'

refused to let the experts from the Kildare Street Museum do any excavations, nor would he have a couple of skeletons found in one of the walls removed, saying that no doubt someone had had good reason to put them there. The metaphorical expression 'skeletons in the cupboard' takes on a fresh vibrancy when they are physically there, set into the wall. My grandparents did, however, initiate further investigations off their own bat. A steward's room was discovered in the basement, where a posse of men sent to arrest one of the O'Carrolls were assassinated, it is said, while their officer was despatched by his host at the dining table on the floor above. The presence of quantities of human bones would seem to verify this sombre episode, which has surfaced in various forms in Leap folklore. The same investigations extended to the Bloody Chapel, and the loveliest of the windows, facing east and said, unconvincingly, to have doubled as the altar, was unblocked. The whole of the 'chapel' was put into a state of preservation to allay the spectre of a particularly repulsive murder, said to have occurred there that gave rise to its epithet of 'bloody'. Nearly a century later, Peter Bartlett arranged for a Mass to be celebrated in the castle to expiate this crime.

The details vary but the story is that in the mid-sixteenth century Thady O'Carroll, brother of the priest at the altar in this room, slew him at prayer for starting to say Mass before he arrived. I trust that this was not One-Eyed Thady who went to see Henry VIII, and was himself murdered by William the Pale in 1553. In some versions of the tale, a massacre followed in which several hundred innocent companions of the murderer and his victim, as well as another local chief who had been worshipping at the service, were done to death. This story is also told of a different chapel in the area, Killistritsa, but its attribution to Leap would explain the spate of real or imagined consequences that have passed into the family's legacy of collective horror and guilt. The stories, once let loose, have never gone away.

The action of murdering someone at prayer, particularly if that person is a priest, represents the ultimate in wickedness; human bestiality extinguishing human spirituality. It is a recurring event in drama as well as in history and legend. Hamlet considers despatching his uncle in just this way, while St Thomas à Becket is the classic substantiated victim. In Irish historical tradition, Brian Boru is said to have avenged the murder of his brother in the late-tenth century by slaying the culprit, the Christian king Imar of the Ostmen, in the sanctuary of the monastery on Scattery Island. In our times Oscar Romero, Catholic

Archbishop of El Salvador, was shot while saying Mass in 1980. So many Leap stories have a universal ingredient that it is my instinct to treasure them as folk tales, rather than to treat them as fact or dismiss them as lies. All that is certain is that the ruined chamber known as the chapel at the summit of the keep is 'bloody' to this day, though it emanates now only a lofty serenity as birds fly in and out of its graceful windows and build their nests in murky crevices.

Some of the hidden spiral staircases also came to light at this time of restoration. My grandmother, Milly Darby, the chatelaine, who was interviewed around the turn of the century by a reporter, was said in the ensuing newspaper article to have been enthralled by the shiny surfaces of the beautifully laid, generous steps and the central columns of these stairways. No doubt they evoked in her novelist's mind visions of generations of blond giants and their ladies hurrying about their business. They would have needed to proceed with care, for the steps were of varying width and depth, to foil intruders.

The cellars and dungeons, some of which had already been investigated by earlier Darbys before coming under Milly's and Jonathan's scrutiny, were cleared of numerous human bones which were carted away and given a Christian burial; and coins of the realm of Edward the Confessor were reputedly found, which makes one wonder whether the foundations are indeed earlier than the modern experts think. Where are those coins now, and who can vouch for their having been found at Leap? Were they minted in the mind of some embellisher or melted in the fire? If only the Kildare Street experts had been allowed a hand in the proceedings! Like the over-enthusiastic archaeologist Heinrich Schliemann[7] at Troy and Mycenae, the Darbys may have destroyed as much evidence as they uncovered.

To get back into the chronology: in about 1750, roughly a century after it had passed, to put it kindly, into Darby hands, Leap underwent a face-lift. The owner at that time was Jonathan Darby the Fifth, who married, in 1745, Susannah Lovett whose parents were both cousins of Sir Edward Lovett Pearce,[8] a celebrated Anglo-Irish architect noted in particular for his designs for Parliament House in Dublin, built between 1729 and 1739. Susannah may well have been influential in the matter of the 'improvements'. It was the time when neo-Gothicism in its early form, known as 'Gothick', was fashionable, Horace Walpole having

7 1822–90.

8 He was in fact dead at the time of his cousin's marriage into the Darby family.

built Strawberry Hill at Twickenham a little earlier, in 1747. Either side of the keep, two stuccoed balancing wings were thrown out, north and south, and the entrance was moved to face west, defensive requirements having been superseded by aesthetic ones. The changed aspect of the imposingly prestigious edifice was further emphasised by the insertion, in its west face, of a beautiful Venetian-style doorway with slender columns and flanking windows in the style of Batty Langley, an architect even more in vogue than Sir Edward Lovett Pearce, and the author of *Gothic Architecture Restored and Improved*, published in 1741.The doorway, complete with its oak door, survives to this day, having somehow escaped burning or theft, and it is on the steps outside it that the wedding group of my parents was photographed. It is thought that the design of the wings was also taken from Langley's pattern book, much used at the time by the socially ambitious participants in the Protestant Ascendancy. Upwardly mobile, they would be called today. Appearances, as always with colonists, were enormously important, and this, combined with the flowering of good architectural taste that characterised the Age of Elegance, resulted in a proliferation of prestige building in Ireland unrivalled elsewhere. Leap was no dazzlingly perfect pile when the Darbys had done, but it did have a charm of its own; hybrid, because the keep, even when castellated into a parody of its former self, resolutely refused to be tamed. Other castles in Ireland, such as Malahide, County Dublin, and Leixlip, County Kildare, received similar treatment, each retaining a compromised identity that somehow came off, none more successfully than Leap. The building is described in 1803 in *The Post Chaise Companion, or Traveller's Directory through Ireland,* as 'a most beautiful seat, and fine castle, with noble and extensive demesnes, plantations and walks, belonging to Mr. Darby'. Alas! there is no sign now of these alfresco delights. The lofty trees, evident in old watercolours and photographs of the castle, are all gone. Carefully placed for effect and nurtured by generations of Darbys, they stood like gracious sentinels, guardians of the Ascendancy way of life. As such they were abhorred by the local people during and after 'the troubles', and not one stands today.

The new rooms in the wings were a triumph. They were judged in a nineteenth-century guidebook, *The New Handbook of Ireland,* by James Godkin and John Walker, to be 'wonderfully light and airy'.[9] Access to the additional bedrooms was achieved by demolishing the

9 p. 243.

first storey in the keep to expose the vaulted ceiling that supported the upper chamber, and putting in an oak gallery that ran round two sides. This was a typical Gothic Revival feature in keeping with the baronial pretensions of the owners. A fine new staircase in the north wing led up to the gallery; you can see the line of it still on the charred west-facing wall, and hear in your mind the swish of silken dresses as the ladies went up and down, like the angels on Jacob's ladder. Later, in my grandparents' time, the clatter of hunting boots and slither of dogs' paws on polished oak would have been the normal staircase sounds, augmented by the shouts of the family members to each other. I have already mentioned that, in my experience, all Darbys shouted, as if they were out hunting, on a grouse moor in a gale, or, as was often the case, engaged in a family row. Conciliatory by nature, it always fascinated me to observe the enthusiasm with which my Darby relations went into battle with each other at the drop of a hat. In the case of my mother and aunts in conflict, any unwary husband caught in the crossfire was pulverised.

The work at Leap continued under the ownership of the next Darby, also Jonathan and elder brother of Admiral Sir Henry d'Esterre Darby. An east-facing door was inserted opposite the main one, opening onto a small terrace overlooking the beautiful, no longer threatening Slieve Bloom mountains; a view that takes your breath away and gives some credence to the story that John Feehan tells in his lovely book, *The Landscape of Slieve Bloom*:

> Saint Columba, looking out from Slieve Bloom over wood covered foothills to the south east, advised Saint Fintan to go back and remain at Clonenagh, because he saw the Angels of God coming and going over it. We are given the impression that he himself remained on Slieve Bloom.[10]

A house that faces east and west has a peculiar magic, known only to those who have lived in one. The sideways infiltration of the rising and setting sun is a constant reminder of flux, as well as bestowing enchanting accidents of shadow and light, often bathed in gold. If there are mirrors, strange effects occur, ranging from the theatrical to the transcendental, while cut-glass, caught in the intensity of dying sunlight, flames into prismatic glory. Such a house, if you are sensitive to these phenomena, can become the outer shell of your innermost consciousness

10 The Blackwater Press, 1979, p. xi.

and liable to reflect it in what are nowadays called paranormal manifestations. It can become a chalice for your joys or, as all too frequently happened at Leap, a cauldron for your terrors. I have not found that a north-south-facing house harbours such evocative subtleties.

In civilisations where directions are all-important and houses placed with deferential care, my observations would not seem at all odd. The Chinese employ a *feng shui* specialist to advise on exactly how to situate a home in order to make the most of the energy lines that traverse the earth's surface, while the American-Indian shamans, or witch doctors, specify the nature of each direction so that a person may take up a position chosen to meet his or her current requirement. For example, you sit with your back to the east (where the heavens 'rise' to illuminate the earth) if you wish for spiritual guidance. You sit with your back to the west (where the earth 'rises' as the sun sets) if you need courage to take action in an earthly situation. All very practical, and interesting to those of us raised in the Christian tradition, where it is assumed, within their east-west religious edifices, that all influence is absorbed from the front. The shamans would consider Leap with its present aspect to be admirably placed.

In due course the Priest's House, too, was romanticised into a turreted, 'Gothicised' appendage to its parent building, of which it was now a part, because of the new north wing which abutted onto it at right angles. At the time of all this aggrandisement, the Priest's House seems to have been the place where the domestic offices and servants' bedrooms were situated, and this was certainly so in my grandparents' time. The back door, facing north, opened into the basement kitchen regions, from which a rabbit warren of corridors gave access to cellars and storerooms, some of them beneath the old keep, where once there had been been dungeons. Upstairs, the children had a nursery and schoolroom as well as bedrooms in the Priest's House, and my Aunt Patricia recalled creeping in the dark all the way from that part of the building, through the north wing and round the gallery to her mother's bedroom in the south wing. This involved passing a pair of cupboard doors which concealed the huge chimney of the original keep (now back in use in Seán Ryan's living room) which held untold terrors for a small girl already in need of her mother's comforting presence.

It would have been at about the same time as the 'Gothicising' that considerable interior embellishments also took place in keeping with the structural alterations. My mother spoke of a black and white chequered marble floor in the hall which has survived in part and is being restored by Seán Ryan, while the *Tribune* newspaper of 14 February 1925 gives further details of the fine interior, concluding: 'Of many beautiful mantel-pieces, one was valued at £500, and was made in Italy by a famous Italian sculptor. The mantel-pieces were all marble, and ceilings were decorated with ornamental plasterwork.' Johnnie Minchin, the oldest of my Irish cousins and the only one to have been to Leap as a child, remembered being told that the original plaster of the walls was made of lime bound by animal blood, and was so hard that recent bullet marks in the hall, pointed out to him by his grandfather, had scarcely made a dent. Trigger-happy Republican rebels were said to be the culprits in this case.

On the east side of the house, the windows of the two wings overlooking the garden were plain Georgian. Was this a later alteration to a once consistent Gothick look? Was a lady of the house overwhelmed by all that spiky, curly romanticism and hankering for something more 'classical' in her best rooms? Who shall say? The records went up in flames.

At one time Leap was surrounded by a village, very few traces of which are visible today. We do know that there was a small factory there in the late eighteenth century which wove serge, and that the estate had its own water mill on the banks of the Knockarly river where oatmeal was ground. These little industries would have been set up to provide for the needs of the local community and seem not to have lasted very long. Agriculture and stock-raising were the main sources of income from the Leap estate under the Darbys until its demise.

It must have been in the late eighteenth century, too, that the ballroom was built, in keeping with the wings and indicative of how grand the Darbys had become. The dance melodies surely floated far and wide over the green expanses of the countryside and it would be interesting to know whether the musical Irish enjoyed the lilting tunes more than they resented the inequality of their lot, or vice versa. The ballroom, now a private house, is slightly removed from the castle itself, as was often the case with country houses in England as well as Ireland. It was approached by a flight of steps, now gone, and there was probably a covered walkway that could be erected when required, to protect the elegantly apparelled ladies and gentlemen in bad weather. In our dressing-up chest there is a black osprey plume set in a diamanté base that belonged to my grandmother, Milly Darby. I expect she wore it in that ballroom; they were all the rage in her middle years as chatelaine, at the height of the Edwardian era. Milly's huge, shocking pink ostrich-feather fan, mounted on tortoiseshell, must also have been in evidence there – very dramatic. It still smells faintly of old scent. I wonder when the balls stopped? Probably some time before the onset of the Great War, for I heard no mention of them by any member of the family. I do not imagine that they were on a par with the glittering formal *soirées* held in the imposing houses of the very rich. I envisage them as entertainment for country neighbours and visitors from England, rather like the hunt balls of my youth; noisy, boisterous affairs, and great fun. There is a rollicking country ball in Tchaikovsky's opera *Eugene Onegin* that always makes me think of similar festivities at Leap, while the formal one, held in a palace in St Petersburg in the same opera reminds me of those that would have taken place in Ireland in grand houses such as Bessborough.

It would be fascinating to know the exact layout of the rooms in the castle; how the furniture was placed, where the huge mirrors hung. One photograph survives, showing the arrangement of furniture in the hall as well as the predictable presence on the walls of a fox's mask and some antlers. A grandfather clock, a gate-legged table, some chests and a Persian rug on the chequered floor can be made out, and my grandmother, unmistakable in her long tweed skirt, stands at the garden door in an attitude that, in hindsight, is almost unbearably poignant. One day, before long, she would look out on that view, unknowingly for the last time. There are no pictures of the other rooms. In most large Irish houses the furniture and hangings would remain unchanged for generations, particularly if the family was hard up, as the Darbys certainly were latterly. Was it, in its last years, lit entirely by oil lamps? I recall having heard that Leap eventually had gas, manufactured on the premises. That would have appealed to my grandfather, who was fond of machinery though unfortunately ill-equipped by nature to exercise the patience demanded for its operation and maintenance. Tales abound of his motoring disasters and the roars of rage that ensued, and the walls surrounding the castle, which had withstood many an onslaught in their time, bore visible testimony, said my mother, to Jonathan's erratic steering.

When she was in her mid-nineties my mother used to revisit Leap in her thoughts. She spoke of the drawing room; the peacock-blue brocade of some of the hangings, of gilded mirrors,[11] of beautiful chairs

11 Richard White-Spunner, the present owner of Milltown Park, poetically referred to Leap as 'a Castle of Mirrors' and recalls that these were stored in the chapel of that house, together with other furniture after the fire, that had been thrown into some concealing bushes.

and tables, of the red bedroom, and the blue bedroom. There was a library too, and the raspberries-and-cream-coloured dining room with the family portraits came back to her. Dogs, she said, barked in the hall. Then, one day, not long before she died, aged ninety-seven, she walked in memory through the garden, describing the flower borders, the tennis court, the trees, and the old retainers who looked after it all. Her pleasure at these recollections was what held my attention more than the details she recounted with such precision. If only I had listened! So much was still recoverable through her memories. These are now gone forever.

On the night of Sunday 30 July 1922, and on the following night, Leap was blown up with dynamite and burned down. I have the telegram that informed my mother of this. I hold the flimsy paper, with its GPO royal cypher and message in purple capital letters, in my hand. It reads 'LEAP CASTLE COMPLETELY BURNED DOWN YESTERDAY MORNING'. I feel the shock waves that pulsated through my mother's frame in her room at Jules' Hotel in Jermyn Street, London, where she was staying the night. No wonder that she rarely spoke of the burning. It was an end of unimaginable bitterness to the Darbys of Leap; an end not only of what they possessed but, more tragically, of what they were for, their *raison d'être*. From stout tower house, chief residence of Irish noblemen, the castle had metamorphosed into the elegant and capacious dwelling of an alien people who, swept in on the colonial tide of their time, had appropriated Leap and its lands. Now it was the charred shell of both its past lives.

4
The New Owners, the Old Stories

PART ONE: THE GREAT ROMANCE

Having explored the structure of Leap Castle from its erection as a tower house at the end of the fifteenth century until the time of its burning, we must take up the story of the people who lived there after the eviction of the O'Carrolls.

It will be recalled that it was not until 1667 that a Darby was firmly in occupation at Leap, following the confusion in which the O'Carrolls lost and regained it, only to encounter final defeat in circumstances that are not entirely clear. It must, however, be reiterated here that according to Darby folklore which was long accepted as the truth, the castle had been in Darby hands since 1558. The story, with some variations, goes as follows.

In that year, in the reign of Queen Mary Tudor, Captain John Darby, the son of a gentleman, Edmund Darby of Gaddesby in Lincolnshire, is part of a force under the Lord Justice, the Earl of Sussex, which takes Leap. Shortly afterwards it is repossessed by the O'Carrolls. So far the story is substantiated in *The Annals of the Four Masters*, but without mention of Captain Darby. In one of the family accounts, Darby is taken prisoner and locked in a cell at the top of the castle. It falls to Finola O'Carroll, the daughter of the house, to push his food through the bars, in the course of which the two fall in love. Having overheard her brother planning a violent death for the young Englishman, Finola manages to get hold of the cell key and releases him, whereupon he races down the spiral staircase, only to encounter the brother on the way up. The Captain turns tail, flees up to the battlements and hurls himself into an adjacent yew tree,[1] from which he clambers down and escapes. He is recaptured and pardoned at the impassioned behest of Finola.

1 Oddly, the yew tree is both a symbol of immortality and the provider of wood for the bow, an instrument of death, and hence is commonly found both in churchyards and in the environs of ancient castles. The Leap one is said to have stood, in much battered shape, until the middle of this century.

There is another version of the escape. In this, the two are waylaid by the brother on the stairway and leap together into the tree, to return in triumph when the castle falls to the English, and Leap and its lands are accorded to Captain Darby as a reward for his services, whereupon he marries Finola. A different ending, with a face-saving slant to it, is that in due course, when hostilities cease, Captain Darby returns to claim his bride, who is now heiress to Leap and its lands.[2] His death, in this record, is in 1604, and his tombstone, bearing this date, is confidently asserted by the Darbys (and in newspaper accounts) to be in the churchyard at Aghancon. There is no sign of it today. Captain Darby is succeeded, in this version of the story, by his reprobate son, known as the 'Wild Captain', who is the subject of his own tale. Yet another account has the two lovers escaping down a secret passage, which links the story into myth. Ariadne, for example, leads imprisoned Theseus to safety down a secret passage in the Cretan tale of the Minotaur. We know that there was a tunnel from Leap to the outside world, a convenient fact to lend authenticity to this pleasing detail, with its dark and hazardous undertones.

When I first started writing this book, it had never occurred to me that what I had known from childhood might not be true. No one, certainly in recent times, had any intention of deceiving historians or themselves; it was a case of being prey to a kind of family propaganda machine. All the tales of Leap – the murders, the love story, the ghosts, the family dramas – were true for us and our parent Darbys simply because we had heard them so often. They were well-known facts.

Much the most important tale was, of course, that of Finola O'Carroll and Captain Darby. This one was often selected by my mother, Diana, from her repertoire of Leap stories when her lady friends came to tea on winter evenings, and we children, formally attired in clean outfits for our customary hour 'downstairs', were part of the audience. Diana was a born raconteur. My sister says she quickly tired of this story because our mother was, by implication, pointing out how much superior her family was to that of our father, but for me it never palled. I would listen avidly, pitying those scented ladies in cloche hats, puffing aromatic cigarettes in shagreen holders. Poor things, they didn't have princes and princesses, castles and kingdoms in their families. Our mother was so grand in my eyes that humbler origins were unthinkable. You had only to look at her long, regal feet.

2 In almost all written accounts, Captain Darby gets Leap as a 'marriage portion'.

Embarking upon the re-telling of this part of the story of Leap, I quickly got into difficulties. It was given in outline in Thomas Lalor Cooke's second *History of Birr*,[3] and included in the fourth edition (but not in earlier ones) of Burke's *Irish Family Records* in 1954. However, Finola and the Captain's romance and marriage in the mid-sixteenth century simply did not fit in with the information that I had unearthed about the O'Carrolls. Could these chroniclers have got the dates wrong? I spent fruitless hours moving this lady of Leap up and down the ladder of time and around its dark corridors, only to find that she fitted in nowhere. Finola floated in space like a lady in a Chagall painting, the green damask gown and anachronistic wimple in which I have pictured her from childhood wafting round her. It did not occur to me that she might never have existed. Captain Darby fared no better. He certainly was not given Leap Castle and its lands as a reward for military service under the Earl of Sussex and the crown of Mary Tudor, for records prove that the O'Carrolls were there for at least three generations after it fell to the Earl. So the Captain, too, was at large, galloping round my mind on his snorting charger, searching for a destination.

Eventually, in despair of ever finding a logical slot for them, I formed a naive, not utterly implausible picture of Finola, the Captain and their offspring, having married soon after the castle's brief surrender to the Earl of Sussex in 1558, huddled in a cramped apartment in the castle rather as a modern couple might occupy the front room of their parents' home in a time of housing shortage. Perhaps Sir William the Pale, traditionally the father of Finola, had taken a fancy to the young Englishman after the defeat and its romantic outcome. Perhaps the eldest son, an obstreperous youth, was spoiled by his grandfather and grew into the Wild Captain, of whose wickedness I have yet to write. I never really believed any of this, but what else was I to do with these two lovebirds, who had perched so beguilingly, side by side, on the topmost twig of the family tree until now?

What I could not do was let the lovers go without a struggle. Perhaps there was some other, more plausible niche in history where the marriage could have taken place, at some quite other point in the story. Maybe the circumstances were not so romantic, and the story was later improved upon. Supposing the romance happened after Cromwell's soldiers attacked the castle, and was subsequently moved back in time?

3 Published posthumously in 1875, p. 218.

After all, who wants a Roundhead in the family if they can have a glamorous Tudor Captain of Horse? Supposing, for the time being, we move the story from 1558 to 1664: what then? This is how things might work out, within the framework of real facts, as opposed to the 'well-known' ones, so faithfully documented, regardless of possibility.

Oliver Cromwell's troops, including an officer named Jonathan Darby, take the castle in 1659, having threatened to attack it with cannon, which it could not have withstood. Darby accepts the place and its lands in lieu of pay and John Carroll and his conjectured daughter Finola are evicted.

In 1664, the anglicised and time-serving John Carroll has his property restored to him. Seeing the way things are going in the confusion following the Restoration, he offers his daughter Finola's hand in marriage to the Roundhead, Jonathan Darby, who, as we saw in chapter 2, had just been evicted from Leap. In this way, the property reverts painlessly to the English, who would have got it back anyway before long, thinks Carroll, and at the same time he gets Finola off his hands. All this would fit in with the established facts. By 1667 'Jonathan Darby of the Leape' was the first of a long line known to have lived there. A pity about the dungeon, the flight, the leap from the battlements and the romantic reunion, but we must forgo these; a cheap price to pay for retaining the possibility of descent from the colourful O'Carrolls through the lovely Finola in her obsolete wimple.

For my part, I can live with this far-fetched hypothesis about the O'Carroll-Darby alliance, just as I could live, at a pinch, with the idea of them sharing Leap with the Captain's 'in-laws' in Tudor times. I cannot eradicate them from the story of Leap as it exists for me. But supposing the whole story turns out, one day, in the face of facts so far hidden from us, definitely to have been invented? Why was it needed? Inventions arise to meet needs. Perhaps it arose, almost by spontaneous combustion, to assuage guilt: conqueror's guilt.

The castle is one of the most powerful symbols we have. It has featured in stories since time immemorial and is at the centre of many of our most widely known fairy tales. It represents the power to repel, the inaccessible, the guardian of an essence, such as a king, a princess, or a precious object like the Holy Grail. Poets have used it as the emblem of virginity, to be captured by the power of love, should the lady be prepared to yield. Edmund Spenser, himself an English official in Ireland in the late-sixteenth century without noticeably more political vision than his contemporaries, wrote his huge allegorical poem *The Faerie*

Queene[4] in Ireland and filled it with castles,[5] inhabited by a galaxy of damsels who either let down the drawbridge voluntarily, were won over by the power of good, or were peremptorily taken by storm by evil doers. The castles of Ireland were certainly in his mind's eye. He himself lived in such a place from 1580 to 1589; Kilcolman Castle in County Cork.

To be deprived of your castle by superior forces must have been a shattering as well as a shameful experience, akin to rape. Anyone who has lived in a commandeered home knows something of the unease this engenders in the victorious occupiers. As a soldier's bride in the Army of Occupation in Germany, shortly after the last European war, my distress to discover that the owner of our 'married quarter' was a concert pianist who had taken up residence in her own garden shed impelled me, against all the anti-fraternisation rules, to knock timidly on the shed door, proffer cigarettes and coffee, and invite her, in schoolgirl German, to come and play on her two grand pianos that graced our sitting-room. She spat at me. Light years the wiser, I told no one. I started to put a few provisions by the shed, furtively, at night.These she took: in those dark days, enemy artists starved as painfully as enemy artisans, and the conquering heroes understandably said 'Serve them right'. I felt no better. I had envisaged a friendship springing up between us, and used to dream of this. Guilt was not to be so easily assuaged.

Had I been a remotely sensitive English usurper, even a Roundhead, with Leap the prize for victory, I would have jumped at the chance to marry the beautiful (of course) blonde daughter of the defeated princeling to ease my conscience; it is such a neat little tale that even if it never happened, it was eventually supposed to have occurred, and doubtless made the Darbys feel better about the way they came by the place. Perhaps in years to come my descendants will take up their embroidery needles and tell how the concert pianist came nightly to her snatched home and filled the air with the strains of Bach and Beethoven while crusty British officers listened, rapt, with tears in their eyes, and glances of understanding passed between the occupying woman and the evicted one. This would be true to the Darby tradition of improving a good story.

It is interesting to note that it was my grandparents who started the fashion of giving each of their children, with the exception of little

4 First printed by William Ponsonbie, in London, and dedicated to Queen Elizabeth, in 1596.

5 There are more than 200 lines describing The Castle of Temperance in *The Faerie Queene*.

Richard,[6] the name O'Carroll. Could it be that at this time of 'Gaelic Revival', of which we shall hear more, the Darbys, keen to get in on the act, resurrected the Finola story and added to it? My grandmother, Milly Darby, was, after all, a novelist.

PART TWO: THE WILD CAPTAIN

Captain John Darby of Leap, said to be the husband of Finola O'Carroll, appears to be as legendary as she. The first Jonathan Darby, supposedly their son, was in fact nothing of the sort; we have seen that he was almost certainly a Cromwellian soldier, but in the fable he is known as the Wild Captain, the epitome of wickedness. He is famed in Darby folklore for one particularly spine-chilling escapade. There is a wealth of variation in the details, as in most Leap stories, but not in the main narrative which I will now relate.

During his tenure of the castle, this Jonathan was accused of high treason and summoned to Birr for his trial. Before the Lord Justice's men arrived to escort him, he sent for his two most trusted retainers and between them the three men collected all the money and valuables held in the castle and, at dead of night, hid the lot within the fortress wall. Then, as dawn broke and the clatter of hoofs in the distance heralded the arrival of the officers of the law, Jonathan climbed onto the parapet of the roof and sent one of the servants to fetch his sword. Alone with the other trusty, Jonathan seized him and hurled him over the battlements. When the messenger returned with the sword his master slew him with it and disposed of him in the same way, so that the Captain's secret was known only to himself.

On his arrest, Jonathan was taken to Birr, tried, found guilty, and thrown into prison, pending execution. He was reprieved on several occasions and at length set free, but his legs, which had been held in irons, had by this time become paralysed and his mind was quite gone except in respect of his buried hoard. On returning home, he could only murmur 'My treasure, my treasure!', and had no idea where he had concealed it.[7] The Wild Captain was later believed to haunt the castle

6 This omission could be significant; Milly may not have immersed herself in the legend in the earliest days of her marriage.

7 It was reported in *The Times* on 22 March 1995, in an article on purchasing houses, that 'The first castle that the Thompsons bought was Cloghan Castle in Banagher, Co. Offaly in 1972 ... When the Thompsons bought the castle the stone walls were in a terrible state because the previous occupant thought they contained gold and spent much of

grounds, peering into crevices in the walls and wringing his hands, his atrophied legs having evidently regained their mobility on his translation to the spirit world.

There is not one scrap of evidence to support this story, but it seems possible that it in fact concerned an O'Carroll. It is quite in keeping with their way of solving a problem, the blood-thirstier ones that is, and the Darbys do seem to have driven out the O'Carrolls while at the same time reaching back to clutch at the latter's identity, borrowing colour from the past rather as the new owners of stately homes buy old portraits to hang on the walls. If they invented Finola, or perhaps dragged her out of the wings into the centre of the stage, why not move the Wild Captain upstage too? There is no reason to suppose that there was anything wild about the Darbys, although they could be ruthless when the occasion demanded. There is a bill extant, presented to a government official for the sum of one shilling and threepence, for 'Hooks for hanging ye rebels' and no doubt the Darby of the time got credit for upholding the law. Sundry executions took place near the castle at a spot known as Hangman's Hill and one of the infamous hooks was found in a tree felled there quite recently. However, it does not matter in the context of this saga that the tale of the Wild Captain is without historical foundation. It has authenticity of a different kind, that of myth. A myth is not an actual event, but represents what is going on all the time. A myth keeps manifesting itself in human experience, and in the case of this one, it actually did so within the family.

My cousin John Minchin, the son of Aunt Cecily (Cis), the second of my grandparents' three daughters, was an only child, very handsome and a favourite of his grandfather. He told me the following story.

Johnnie, as he was known to us, was about six when Jonathan and Milly Darby came to stay with their daughter and her first husband Ted Minchin at their house in Westmeath, because their own home, Leap Castle, had been burned down. One day Johnnie's grandfather gave him a five pound note, telling him in a whisper to keep quiet about it. The little boy, overwhelmed by the size and frailty of the old-fashioned fiver, slipped down to the village post office, where he got the postmistress to change it into the more maneagable and substantial units of

---

her time digging holes in them. "She didn't find anything and neither have I," says Mr Thompson.' There is an irresistible echo in this story of the Wild Captain and his lost treasure, buried in an O'Carroll castle in the same county. Perhaps the myth of treasure at Cloghan Castle was directly borrowed from that of Leap or both stories sprang from a much older one, adapted to fit the particular historical circumstances of the castle in question.

half crowns. These he took home and buried in the garden. A few days later, his nanny called him to her side and asked him sternly where he had got the money that the postmistress had reported him to have changed into silver at her counter. Johnnie was too frightened to prevaricate. Sobbing, he told Nanny that his grandfather had given it to him as a present. Jonathan Darby was not famed for benevolence or generosity, and the woman was convinced that her charge was lying. The child, however, stuck to his guns, and she was obliged to seek an audience (it really was like that) with my grandfather to check the story. 'What happened then?' I asked Johnnie. 'She never said another word about it,' he replied, 'I expect he told her to go to hell!'

Johnnie crept out into the garden later that day to recover his treasure. He never found it. Anxiety had driven its whereabouts out of his mind. The myth had repeated itself – the agent in this case an innocent child, the motive, as in the old story, fear. Carl Jung called this sort of thing synchronicity; meaningful coincidence.

What are these two tales really about? On the surface they illustrate the squirrel instinct we all have, which itself is prompted by a need to be prepared for lean times. All sorts of little hoards turn up in the houses of the old. I think, however, that at a deeper level these tales of hidden treasure represent the universal human tendency to bury our anxieties and then become distressed because we cannot locate and deal with them.

The fabric of the saga of Leap is shot through with gleaming threads of possibility; metallic, tarnishable thread, jostling the good warp and weft of serviceable fact, lifting it from the practical, endowing it with the glint of creativity, like a pop star's jacket. A little embroidery here and there is also evident. Historians may unpick it if they are so inclined, and discard the tinselly strands in the material. My aim is to present the story of the place and its people as it has come down to me, not in a spirit of indiscriminate credulity, but honouring the whole, even when the suspension of disbelief must operate if the tale is to be told with respect. The buried 'treasure' of the endangered Wild Captain and that of the solitary child in a world full of grown-ups beckon to each other across the centuries.

We must now return to the Darby family tree, and to what is known to have happened.

5
The Darbys of Leap

In the previous chapter I presented two hypotheses about the alleged O'Carroll-Darby union, from the biased angle of one who cherishes, against all the odds, the possibility of that alliance. I make no apology for stretching credulity almost to snapping point. That done, we must now address the facts.

John Darby, at the top of the family tree as drawn up by Burke in 1954 (but not, interestingly, in earlier editions), seems, on the evidence available, never to have existed. Sadly, this also removes his bride, Finola O'Carroll, from her time-honoured place at his side. She has to be relegated to the part of leading lady in the acquisition myth propagated by descendants of the *parvenu* Darby settlers, a myth obscuring the unpalatable truth that they almost certainly obtained the place not in Tudor times but by force of arms between 1649 and 1659. In fact, as already noted in chapter 2, the first mention of a 'Jonathen' Darby of 'Leape' occurs in the poll tax account of 1659. Finola's son, the Wild Captain, is by the same token inadmissible to the pedigree. We have to accept that the first Darby to live at Leap was Jonathan Darby, a Cromwellian settler,[1] ignoring the allegations made by some genealogists, based on family tradition.

I have described the first Darbys of Leap as *parvenus,* and I seem to hear the rattle of angry bones from the churchyard at Aghancon, on the Leap estate, where so many of them are buried. Perhaps the old Darbys will settle again when I explain that it is merely their origins, not their lofty social standing over many generations in the country of their adoption, that concern me here, for we shall see that there is no evidence to connect them with the old landed Darbys of Gaddesby, whom they claimed as their forebears. I would not go so far as the magnificently insulting poet O'Bruadair, who, with a large measure of poetic licence, lumped all the Cromwellian settlers together as '...the dregs of

1 *Calender of State Papers, 1660–1662.*

each base trade, who range themselves snugly in the houses of the noblest chiefs, as proud and genteel as sons of gentlemen'.[2] Nevertheless, the fact must be faced that my Anglo-Irish ancestors were not as noble as they originally declared and subsequently believed themselves to be.

The Darbys of Gaddesby, in Lincolnshire, had arrived at that place by 1377, according to local Poll Tax records, in which they feature as de Derby. They became lords of the manor of Gaddesby, and their descendants have fine tombs and memorial plaques in the neighbouring church of Rothley. They ceased to be so after one Libeus Darby, in Tudor times, failed to have a son, and so the estate passed to his daughter.[3] However, it will be recalled that according to my recent Darby ancestors (who also embraced the fanciful notion that the family were of Norman extraction and originally called D'Arby), it was in 1558 that John Darby, son of one Edmund Darby of Gaddesby, went to Ireland in the Earl of Sussex's force, married the O'Carroll heiress to Leap Castle on its surrender and was granted the place for his own. There is no mention in the Gaddesby records of an Edmund or of John, his putative son, which argues for the probability that he was an invention.[4] It was not at all uncommon for settlers in Ireland to claim kinship with distinguished families of the same name living in England, to give themselves added social standing in their new milieu, and that is probably what happened with the Darbys of Leap.

Out of the genealogical confusion, clarity begins to dawn with the dates on the gravestones, at Aghancon church, of Jonathan Darby of Leap and his wife Deborah, who died in 1685 and 1688 respectively. He is the second of the long line of Jonathans, presumably the son of the first. Why did this repetition of the name Jonathan persist? Perhaps the Darbys felt that a handed down Christian name gave them a sense of heritage, part of their identity as landed gentry, and then, after three or four Jonathans, they became locked into a comfortable tradition. No doubt the inheritance of the name as well as the place was also a constant reminder of a landlord's duties, in much the same way as the

2 *Poems of David O Bruadair, 1625–1698*, ed. J. C. MacErlain (1917).

3 A. H. Thompson, in *Transactions*, vol. 13, p. 263. 1921–2.

4 It should, however, be noted that one 'John Derby' is listed among the forty-nine officers who returned from exile with their monarch, Charles, in 1659, having been banished by Cromwell for their Royalist sympathies. This band of men were styled 'The Protestant Royalist Officers who had served the King before 1649'. I do not discount the possibility that this 'John Derby' could have been connected to the Gaddesby family, and could have married an O'Carroll heiress to one of the other clan properties and been duly annexed by the Leap folklorists.

declamatory repetition of O'Carroll history by the Ollamhs to each succeeding Prince of Ely had drawn attention to their obligations. It was part of the bargain for plantation families, whether they acquired their property by force of arms or other means, that they should assume responsibility for it under the Crown, rendering the land more productive and such native Irish as remained more docile. This was no mean undertaking in view of the sporadic risings and ongoing resentment of the conquered.

Part of the difficulty lay in the vast culture gap between the new English and the Anglo-Norman inhabitants. Most of the latter had intermarried with the host nation, adopting their ways, even though from time to time the more powerful of them had served the English. When they saw their lifestyle and their power threatened by invasions subsequent to the one that had brought them to the country, they joined forces with the indigent population. 'More Irish than the Irish' was how they came to be known. There was, generally speaking, no 'hail fellow, well met' between the old English and the new arrivals; far from it.

Another obstacle to peaceful co-existence was that the English settlers in the seventeenth century saw the native Irish as in some respects virtually pagan, with a contemptible culture, ignoring their capacity for learning. For instance, some Irish people knew the Roman authors and wrote and spoke Latin (an accomplishment doubtless initiated in part by the Latin Masses of the Catholic church services) while the Irish language embraced subtleties of thought that were mystifying to the conquerors, as was their bardic tradition and respect for Brehon law, the system in use in Gaelic Ireland.[5] By the time the Darbys were installed at Leap, most of the more educated local people would have spoken English as their second language – in fact we have seen that the O'Carroll nobles communicated with the Crown officials in that tongue in late Tudor times. However, Gaelic continued to be widely used and was associated with resistance. We can assume that there was not much of a language problem for the Darbys since they would have had their own people in positions of authority, but it was incumbent upon them from the start to 'civilize' their territory as part of their brief, and from the time that their activities started to be recorded the Darbys emerge as efficient colonists in the repressive climate of their times; conscientious and industrious, later becoming kindly and concerned for the welfare of their underlings.

5 R. F. Foster, *Modern Ireland 1600–1972*, ch. 1, 'Wild Shamrock Manners'.

That some of the Irish, including those few Carrolls who had survived and remained in their land, made rings round the settlers intellectually, confusing them with sophistry and outwitting them with wiliness, must have made the early Darbys, if they were as forthright as most of their descendants seem to have been, uneasy to say the least. It may well have started the Darbys' habit of conducting all conversations at a shout, for which, as I have already indicated, many are famed to this day.

Jonathan and Deborah's son, Jonathan, comes next in line of succession. He was appointed High Sheriff of the King's County in 1674[6] but was unfortunate in that, being Protestant, he fell foul of King James II's 'Patriot' Parliament, which sought to continue attempts to redress the wrongs inflicted on Catholics by the Cromwellian administration, started in his brother's time. James II called into his service, in pursuance of this aim, certain Irishmen such as Colonel Oxburgh, who had previously held the position of agent to Sir Laurence Parsons at Birr Castle. In doing so, he caused the two, who had previously been associates, to become enemies. This was bound to lead to trouble, and did so in 1688, according to Cooke's *History of Birr*, a most illuminating document, which has an account based on a contemporary written record, since lost, of what happened.

At that time there was much unrest around Birr, with robbers and other desperados, ex-soldiers known as 'rapparees', causing havoc among the people. Sir Laurence's neighbours, including many of his own tenants, besought him to give them shelter within the castle walls. Sir Laurence took pity on them and took in some eighty locals, including the Darbys of Leap, before ordering the gates to be shut against the marauders. Colonel Oxburgh, an opportunist if ever there was one, saw his chance to gain credit with his superiors and reported to the Lord Lieutenant, Lord Tyrconnell, that Sir Laurence held a garrison in the castle against the king, which, upon the charge being investigated at Tyrconnell's request, proved to be false. Nevertheless, Oxburgh stuck to his guns and proceeded, without reference to higher authority, to demand possession of the castle. Sir Laurence declined to obey unless the Lord Lieutenant ordered him to do so, whereupon Oxburgh and one ill-named Colonel Grace besieged and eventually took the castle, arresting, on a series of trumped up charges, a number of the people within, including Sir Laurence himself and Jonathan Darby of Leap, together with his younger brother, John. Jonathan and his brother's

6 *Patentee Officers in Ireland 1173–1826* (ed. Hughes, Dublin, 1960), p. 38.

only offence was that of having rescued a Captain Coote from the king's constables. They were all flung into prison.

Sir Laurence and five of his tenants, together with Jonathan and John Darby and one John Rascoe, were tried on 30 March 1689. The judge charged the jury to find them all guilty of high treason but the only ones to receive that verdict were Sir Laurence, Jonathan Darby, and John Rascoe, presumably because they each had property that could be appropriated at their demise. These three were to be hanged, drawn and quartered, but after several stays of execution during which Parsons was reprieved, the fate of the remaining two still hung in the balance. The long-drawn-out stress of these innocent people is comparable to that of prisoners on Death Row in some American states to this day. Jonathan Darby, languishing in captivity and haunted by the prospect of a most hideous end, may well have wondered if his family's translation into prestigious landowners was really worthwhile.

On 1 July 1690 James II was defeated at the Battle of the Boyne by William of Orange, who was subsequently crowned King of England and reigned jointly with his wife Mary, James's sister. The fortuitous arrival upon Irish soil of victorious, Protestant 'King Billy', so reminiscent of that thrilling scene in Beethoven's opera, *Fidelio,* when the captive hero, Florestan, is saved from death by the sound of the liberators' trumpet outside the gaol, must have seemed like divine intervention to Jonathan Darby, whose own life was saved in the same way, though without the king actually coming to Birr. No wonder the Darbys were to become such enthusiastic Orangemen.

Sir Laurence Parsons was quickly sworn in as High Sheriff of the King's County and as a Commissioner of Affray, or peacekeeper, along with his neighbour Jonathan Darby of Leap and others. Jonathan 'is alleged to have committed many deeds of daring against rapparees'.[7]

Oxburgh, promoted to the post of Provost Marshal to King's County by James II before the latter's defeat and flight, had caused a triple gallows to be erected in the square at Birr on May Day 1689, known thenceforward, with macabre humour, as Colonel Oxburgh's Maypole. He must have been furious that it was never used for his chosen victims, but I am delighted to report that, still according to Cooke, 'his wife and he had a dispute, which ended in their parting beds'. I imagine she could stand the odious man no longer, but she came to a sad end 'after the decline of her fortune', says Cooke, 'and was forced to employ her

7 C. L. Adams, *The Ancient Castles of Ireland* (London, 1904), p. 270.

coach in carrying firewood for sale into Birr'. Piously, he adds: 'A doleful example is this of the instability of human greatness.' I expect that the Darbys bore her no ill will, but it is too much to hope that they might have helped to alleviate her distress.

Jonathan was married some time before 1693, says Burke, to Anna Maria d'Esterre, whose maiden name was given to her great-grandson, Admiral Sir Henry d'Esterre Darby. It was declared in my mother's family that the d'Esterres were of Huguenot origin, and French nobility at that, and the Darbys were not alone in believing this.[8]

In *The Huguenot Settlements in Ireland* by Grace Lawless Lee,[9] the author, quoting from a lost manuscript of 1892, states that 'Henry d'Esterre and his Dutch wife of noble birth, Annie Amy Van Boffear, sailed up the Shannon bringing with them an immense amount of treasure in money, jewels and valuable china and table linen, "enough to supply twenty families"', adding that they 'purchased an estate in County Clare which they named Castle Henry'. In fact, this story is incorrect. Huguenots who fled to Holland after the Edict of Nantes was revoked in 1665, causing their expulsion from France, certainly did go on from there to England and Ireland, but the family we know as the d'Esterres in fact was called Dester, Destar, or De Staar, and were Dutch merchants! They had arrived in Limerick laden, very probably, with all that linen, silver and crockery, some sixteen years before the Edict was revoked. They all read Dutch, and spoke in that language, so we can assume that even if they hailed originally from France, they had lived in Holland for some time. This family of retailers was prominent among some forty others from Holland encouraged to trade in Limerick by Lord Orrery to replace the Catholic merchants who had all been banished after the terrible siege of the town by Cromwell's troops in 1651. When they changed their name to d'Esterre is not known, but Burke states that Abraham and Henry Dester became denizens in 1669, close enough to the flight of the Huguenots for them to jump on that bandwagon, so perhaps they 'became' Huguenot refugees (claiming descent from the Counts of Aix) at the same time as they obtained the right of residence in Ireland. By 1675 they had grown rich enough to rent Rossmanagher Castle from the Earl of Thomond, which they later bought outright and renamed Castle Henry. It stood near the estuary of the River Shannon, not far from the Bunratty river, which is still crossed by d'Esterre's Bridge.

8 It was not unusual for the Irish themselves to 'Frenchify' their names.
9 No. 205 National Library of Ireland Ms 3205.

By 1690 Abraham must have died, for it is his brother or perhaps son, Henry, who is described in that year by Sir Donat O'Brien as 'one of the chief gentlemen and ablest persons of the county'. Henry's ability would no doubt have accelerated his social ascent, set in motion by his family's wealth. His wife, Anna Maria, left in her will ten pounds to her granddaughter, Anna Maria d'Esterre, later, as we have noted, to become the chatelaine of Leap as the wife of the Jonathan Darby who so narrowly escaped the gallows.

This marriage seems to be the sole connecting link between the Darbys and the d'Esterres, but, as part of the family saga, the tale must be told of a distant Darby cousin, John Neville Norcott d'Esterre, a godson of Admiral Henry d'Esterre, who was killed in a duel by Daniel O'Connell,[10] the famous champion of Catholic Emancipation, in 1815. O'Connell had made a disparaging remark about the Dublin Corporation which he refused to withdraw, whereupon the two fought with pistols. O'Connell is said to have deeply regretted killing his opponent. In penitence, he wore a black glove on the hand that pulled the trigger whenever he attended Mass for the rest of his life, and made such amends as he could to d'Esterre's young wife by acting professionally for her in a lawsuit free of charge (he was a barrister) and recovering a large debt.[11]

I hope Jonathan and Anna Maria were happy together. He had suffered greatly at the hands of Colonel Oxburgh, and that must have left its mark, although he went on to do his duty by the County. I see them in my mind's eye sitting contentedly at Leap on summer evenings, when work on the land was finished for the day and the English steward sent home, swapping stories of their families' supposed and real adventures and enjoying such of the Dutch treasures as may have come their way. Two pictures, each described as 'Oil Painting, Dutch Scene' appear in the inventory of contents burned at Leap in 1922, but I would have expected there to be more, since the Dester roots were in trade and it was generally the merchant class in Holland that commissioned the painters, handing the pictures on to their descendants. The later Darbys may not have liked them; one is listed in this inventory among the contents of the schoolroom, a significant relegation.

10 1776–1847.

11 All my information about the d'Esterres comes from *The Irish Genealogist,* vol. 5, no. 6 (November 1979). Article by Esmé Colley.

In *Anthropoid Apes,*[12] a powerful novel by my grandmother, Milly Darby, the weak-minded philanderer who ruins the heroine's life is called d'Esterre. Why did she choose this unusual family name for her anti-hero? Was it to annoy her husband, who disapproved of her literary activities?

This Jonathan was still alive, says Burke, in 1708, and was succeeded at Leap by his son Jonathan, who in 1707 had married Anna Maria Frend. During their time at Leap there was a famine in Ireland that lasted from 1739 until 1741, as a result of which one third of the entire population of one and a quarter million died. This had been caused largely by the ruin of Irish industries by Acts of Parliament in England, which saw its own commerce as under threat from Irish competition. Almost all branches of Irish trade and manufacture were destroyed; the collapse of the wool trade in particular caused untold hardship. For some time the Irish had been prevented from marketing their cattle and pigs to the English colonies and this, combined with the stagnation of almost all other branches of their trade, led to a period of misery in which extreme poverty tipped over into devastating famine. There is no record of how things were at Leap, but this Jonathan Darby was a justice of the peace and, it is to be hoped, a merciful and equitable one in keeping with an already established family tradition. His will is dated 13 December 1742, and his wife is known to have survived him. There is no sign of their graves in the churchyard, nor those of his parents. Why should they have been interred elsewhere? Have their graves simply become obliterated?

Their son, the next Jonathan to succeed to the ownership of Leap and its lands, has a memorial in the church at Aghancon, which tells us that he was born in 1708. He was trained in the law in London, and married Susannah Lovett from Liscombe Park, in Buckinghamshire, in 1745. He died in 1776. These two are buried in the churchyard, and, it will be recalled, were responsible for 'Gothicising' the castle. It is to be hoped that all that building gave employment to the local people – cheap labour, no doubt, but beneficial to all concerned, and badly needed after the preceding lean years.

Jonathan and Susannah's son, predictably yet another Jonathan, was born at Leap in 1746 and followed his father into the law, but having qualified in London he returned to Ireland to attend to his inheritance. It is he who in 1780, under what was called the Volunteer Movement,

12 1909.

raised the Leap Independents, a small private army trained to keep the peace at a time when the usual military forces in Ireland had been for the most part called away to fight the American War of Independence. He commanded them himself, taking the title of Colonel, and issued them with a smart blue uniform, piped with white. He married Eleanor Lovett, his first cousin and a neighbour from County Tipperary, became High Sheriff of King's County, and was one of the people who paid for the building of a new church at Aghancon in 1787,[13] described in *The Post Chaise Companion* of 1803 as 'a beautiful object' and 'an elegant modern Gothic building'. I find it a touch forbidding from the outside, but the simple interior is enhanced by an array of fine memorial tablets to many of the Darbys and their relations.

Jonathan died in 1802, was buried in the churchyard at Aghancon and is commemorated in the church on a tablet which records his kindness as well as his efforts to preserve the peace during the 1798 rebellion, adding that this 'was acknowledged by Protestants and Roman Catholics'. It concludes, 'He died deeply lamented by a very large circle of friends.' Were the Leap Independents disbanded then? It would have been a comfort in uncertain conditions to have one's own private army, though expensive to train and maintain it. Perhaps there was a government subsidy. This Jonathan was a responsible landlord, a loyal servant of the Crown and a force for good. He may well have set an example of public service to his younger brother, Henry d'Esterre Darby, who succeeded him at Leap in 1802, since Jonathan and Eleanor had just one child, a daughter named after her mother. He is the most distinguished by far of Leap's Darby owners.

Henry d'Esterre Darby was born in 1749 and went into the British Navy, which was a not unusual career choice for a landowner's younger son. He was captain of HMS *Bellerophon,* a typical warship of her time with 74 guns, at the Battle of the Nile on 3 August 1798. Henry, in command of 590 sailors, took part with four other of Nelson's captains in a hazardous manoeuvre, sailing through shallows between the French fleet, in the bay of Aboukir, and the land, and demolishing the unsuspecting French almost completely. The *Bellerophon* took on the 120-gun French flagship, *L'Orient* – a gallant action but one she paid dearly for, being dismasted within an hour.[14] She had to be taken out of

13 Sir Charles Coote, *Statistical Survey of the King's County* (1801).
14 *The Times* (3 October 1798).

the battle. Casualties were heavy, and the following letter, in Nelson's own hand, was brought to Henry when the battle was over and won:

> My Dear Darby,
> I grieve for your heavy loss of brave fellows, but look at our glorious Victory. We will give you every assistance so soon as you join us, till then God Bless you, Ever yours faithfully, Horatio Nelson. Aug: 3rd 1798.

A footnote adds: 'We shall both I trust soon get well.' Nelson had been wounded in the head during the battle, but the nature and extent of Captain Henry's wounds is not known.

The Battle of the Nile was indeed a 'glorious victory', saving Britain's territories in India from the threat of Napoleon's army in Egypt. *The Times*[15] is full of it. Under the heading of 'ADMIRAL NELSON'S VICTORY' the announcement opens with the words:

> The official news of the GLORIOUS VICTORY obtained by Admiral Nelson over the French Fleet, near Rosetta arrived at the Admiralty yesterday morning at a quarter past eleven o'clock… The Park and Tower guns, and the merry peals from the steeples of several churches, soon announced this happy news to the public.

The report continues with the publication of a long, exuberant letter from Nelson himself to the Secretary of the Admiralty in which he praises his 'officers and men of every description', adding: 'Could anything from my pen add to the character of the Captains, I would write it with pleasure, but that is impossible.' It is interesting to note that, in those days, news of a victory at sea in the Eastern Mediterranean could take eight weeks to reach London.

In this same edition of the newspaper, notice is given of a 'Grand Gala in honour of Lord Nelson's Glorious Victory' to be held at Ranelagh. Surely something of the kind was organised at Leap, in the ballroom, with Captain Darby, so soon to inherit, as guest of honour? No doubt he would have been given a rapturous welcome, but how heartfelt would that welcome have been amongst the local Catholic Irish? Catholics were not yet emancipated. It was a time of turmoil, with the country, inspired by Wolfe Tone and his 'United Irishmen' making a bid for independence, and the British government cracking down on it, often with over-zealous yeomanry troops, which led to

15 3 October 1798.

massacres and near revolution. In 1800 the hated Act of Union, which abolished the Irish Parliament, would place Ireland in an even more subservient position, reinforcing the Protestant Ascendancy. England's victories, so palatable to the Irish ruling class, may well have tasted bitter to their Catholic underlings. Nonetheless, they had their livelihood to protect, and probably cheered as enthusiastically as their Protestant neighbours when a conquering hero returned to the home of his forefathers.

In 1799 Captain Darby became Admiral Sir Henry d'Esterre Darby, a fine name. His portrait by Sir William Beechey, of which only engravings survive after its destruction in the burning of 1922, does justice to that title in its open countenance, good features and firm yet gentle expression. He died in 1823, an ancestor to be proud of, and a genuine one at that. The neat sequel in later Darby folklore related that Nelson became godfather to Henry's son and that the name Horatio was thenceforth perpetuated in succeeding generations of Darbys. A glance at the family tree would have revealed Admiral Henry's permanent bachelorhood. However, Nelson did make a bequest to his faithful friend Darby of several of his personal possessions, still in the family today, apart from some gifts to Henry during their lifetime. One cherished artefact, 'the Nelson coffee pot', assumed to be lost in the fire or looted, was spotted by my Uncle Douglas in a silversmiths in Bond Street in 1925 on the eve of his marriage to my Aunt Patricia. He gave it to her as a wedding present. The Darbys have also hung onto his Lordship's august name, using it at intervals down to the present day, when Kevin Horatio Martin O'Carroll Darby, great-grandson of the last Darby of Leap, has been the bearer of it since his baptism in 1966. I expect he had to keep quiet about this at school.

Heroines, if there have been any in the Darby family, go unrecorded, and such female Christian names as have been repeated from time to time have been bestowed in love rather than admiration, I would guess, which is perhaps the best reason of all for their perpetuation. As an admirer of my grandmother I would like to hear of a latterday Milly Darby, but in this era no girl would thank her parents for calling her Mildred. No doubt the name, that of an eighth-century saint of royal Anglian blood who became an abbess on the Isle of Thanet, and was regarded as 'a comforter to all in affliction'[16] will come back into fashion one day soon.

16 *Penguin Dictionary of Saints*.

It was to HMS *Bellerophon*, now commanded by Captain Maitland, that Napoleon surrendered after the Battle of Waterloo on 15 July 1815, and that same ship carried him into banishment on St Helena.

Henry d'Esterre Darby's uncle, according to the family tree, was the other Darby admiral, George. He was born around 1720, and had a distinguished naval career, culminating in 1780 as Commander-in-Chief of the Western Squadron and Lord of the Admiralty. There is a full-length, rather paunchy portrait of him by Romney in the Painted Hall at Greenwich. Subsequently he became the Member of Parliament for Plymouth from 1780 to 1784.

Henry himself was a lieutenant on George's flagship, *Britannia*. There is some doubt as to whether they were in fact uncle and nephew for a number of reasons. There is, for instance, no mention of George in the church at Aghancon, which, were he a close relative, would surely not have been so. Many others, of little or no distinction, feature, as I have already said, on imposing bas-relief memorials in that otherwise unadorned building. It seems more likely that George was at most a distant relation, and that it was advantageous to both George and Henry to claim a closer family link; the former for social and the latter for professional reasons. Preferment in the Navy in those days of patronage was frequently boosted by such connections. George is described in the *Dictionary of National Biography* as a 'man of no distinction and very slender abilities', but Captain Constantine Phipps who served under him speaks of his 'manliness and firm sense, which makes him do everything for the best'.[17] If he were indeed some sort of senior cousin, and not the uncle of Henry d'Esterre Darby, as Burke alleges, the socially superior Henry, already the recipient of George's patronage, would hardly dispute his pretensions to a closer relationship to the Darbys of Leap Castle than was in fact the case.[18] In the previously mentioned *New Handbook of Ireland* the writers remark on the similarity of William Henry Darby of Leap to the portrait of his ancestor Henry d'Esterre Darby as follows: 'There is such a strong likeness between this hero and the present proprietor of Leap Castle that the fine old picture of the admiral might easily be taken as his portrait.' No such family look is remarked upon with regard to the portrait of Admiral George which, the writers observe, hangs nearby. The engravings I

17 *The Private Papers of John, Earl of Sandwich, First Lord of the Admiralty 1771–1782*, ed. G. R. Barnes and J. H. Owen, vol. 4 (Navy Records Society, 1938), p.3.
18 See Appendix 4.

have of those two pictures show utterly dissimilar features. For my part, I am glad that George got hitched onto the family at Leap, for that seems to have benefited both Darby seamen, and two family admirals are better than one.

One of Admiral Henry d'Esterre's younger brothers also achieved distinction in the armed forces of the Crown. This was General Christopher Darby, who was born in 1758 and served in the Peninsular War as Colonel of the 54th Regiment of Foot. There was a portrait of the General in the dining room at Leap, by Sir William Beechey; it was lost in the fire with all the others, but another one exists.

When Henry d'Esterre died in 1823 aged seventy-four, he was succeeded by his brother, John Darby of Marklye in Sussex, the third brother in a row. This John had called his eldest son Jonathan in anticipation of his succeeding the Admiral at Leap, but he died at the age of twenty-two in 1809 after attending Christ Church, Oxford, studying for the bar (he was admitted to Lincoln's Inn at the early age of seventeen). Jonathan was evidently one of those too good to be true people, for his memorial tablet in the church at Aghancon, where he is buried in the churchyard, says of him 'He lived a rare example of Virtue. He died a rare example of resignation: in both Religion was his Ruling principle.' Resignation is unfashionable: it has a gloomy ring about it today. Acceptance, which implies an act of the will, is more in keeping with contemporary attitudes.

It would have been a harsh blow to Admiral Henry to lose his eldest nephew just seven years after his own inheritance of Leap. Henry was sixty at the time of young Jonathan's death. His brother John, who succeeded him, was not much younger. He was married to Anne Vaughan, of Welsh descent, in 1784, and they had five surviving sons and three daughters. He appears to have made over his Sussex property, Marklye, to his son George,[19] who married four years after his father had inherited the castle. In 1827 the school at Aghancon was built by John Darby, with local assistance, but little else is known of his short tenure at Leap. He is registered as living in Great George Street, Westminster from 1800 until 1834, the year of his death, so perhaps he was not often in Ireland, although some of his children studied there. It would not have been easy for him or for his wife to adapt, at their ages, to an alien culture and so different a way of life after years in London and Sussex. They had some devoutly religious children, the most notable of these being their youngest son, John Nelson Darby, who was born in

19 Burke.

1800. Although by no means in the direct line of descent, he was such a remarkable figure and has exerted so lasting an influence on the Evangelical movement within the Christian Church that I must give him an honoured place in these pages.

Having graduated from Trinity College, Dublin as a Classical Gold Medallist in 1819 and been called to the Irish Bar in 1822, John Nelson Darby relinquished his promising legal career in 1825 to enter the Church. He was ordained deacon and given the curacy of the Calary district in the Wicklow Mountains. In 1826 he was ordained priest, but shortly afterwards he was injured in a riding accident. He spent the best part of 1827 convalescing at the home of his much older sister, Susan Pennefather, a godly woman whose spirituality doubtless reinforced his own. He recovered completely from his disability and was later famous for his powerful physique until well into his old age, though this seems not to have been the case at the time when Francis William Newman, brother of the Cardinal, wrote of John Nelson Darby under the title of 'The Irish Clergyman':

> This was ... a most remarkable man, who rapidly gained an immense sway over me. I shall henceforth call him 'The Irish Clergyman'. His bodily presence was indeed weak.[20] A fallen cheek, a bloodshot eye, crippled limbs resting on crutches, a seldom shaven beard, a shabby suit of clothes, and a generally neglected person, drew at first pity, with wonder to see such a figure in a drawing room. It has been reported that a person in Limerick gave him a penny, thinking him to be a beggar, and if not true, this story was well invented... He became an indefatigable curate in the mountains of Wicklow. Every evening he sallied forth to teach in the cabins, and roving far and wide over mountains, amid bogs, was seldom home before midnight. By such exertions, his strength was undermined and he so suffered in his limbs that not lameness only but yet more serious results were feared... He made me more and more ashamed of political economy and moral philosophy, and all science, all of which ought to be counted dross for the excellency of the knowledge of Christ Jesus our Lord... Never before had I seen a man so resolved that no word of the New Testament should be a dead letter to him.

In 1827 John Nelson Darby, this man with so strong a calling,

20 A reference to St Paul in II Corinthians 10.10.

resigned his priesthood. There was a new movement in the air, which had begun as early as 1812 in New York, with a small group of people meeting to celebrate their faith and to worship God without the constraints of established ritual. In the early decades of the nineteenth century a similar movement arose in Ireland, at first among intellectuals and the prosperous Anglo-Irish, towards what they saw as the true Christianity. It offered John Nelson all that he had found lacking in the coldly formal established Church. Increasingly sceptical as to the validity of this Church and deploring in particular its lax adherence to the scriptures, John Nelson Darby joined 'The Brethren', a group recently founded by A. N. Groves and a few others in Dublin. Proclaiming the priesthood of every believer, they rejected all clergy, all ceremonial, including the Communion Service as laid down in the Prayer Book, and all other outward forms of worship. They saw themselves as brothers in Christ.

John Nelson very quickly became an influential member of the brotherhood, which started rapidly to expand. In 1827 he issued his first pamphlet, 'The Nature and Unity of the Church of Christ', which caused something of a furore in the Protestant churches and swelled the ranks of the Brethren. In it, he wrote:

> Am I desiring believers to correct the Churches? I am beseeching them to correct themselves, by living up, to the same measure, to the hope of their calling... Let them testify against the blindness and secularity of the Church, but let them be consistent in their own conduct.

No wonder the established Church was discomfited. It was in any event not in a very strong position, representing a mere one eighth of the population of Ireland.

In 1830 John Nelson visited Paris, Cambridge and Oxford, where he met Benjamin Wills Newton who invited him to preach at Plymouth, where the first congregation was formed in 1831. They met at Providence Chapel in that city, and henceforth were known as Plymouth Brethren, which name displeased them but nevertheless stuck.

It was in about 1836 that disagreements arose among the faithful. There was dissent about whether each meeting should be a law unto itself or whether all assemblies should be centrally controlled. It was felt by many, including Groves himself, that to centralise was to depart from the fundamental principles of the sect. Difficulties also arose over the chosen procedure for worship, which consisted of just two events, the sharing of bread and wine and the voicing of spiritual insights by members of the congregation, any of whom might address the assembly. The absence of officiating clergy and almost total lack of structure inevitably led to abuses of the ideals of the Brethren by those who liked the sound of their own voices and could not resist assuming a leader's role, albeit with the best intentions. The sharing of the bread and wine, initially the heart of the meetings, was soon in second place, after the perorations. This was a departure from Darby's vision of Divine Service, based on early Christianity as exemplified in the Bible.

Between 1838 and 1840 John Nelson worked in Switzerland. His lectures were enthusiastically received, particularly in the cantons of Geneva, Berne and Vaux, where a number of congregations soon flourished. The local Jesuits were angered by this outbreak of fundamentalism and in 1845 their intrigues provoked an uprising in Vaux, during which Darby's followers were persecuted. In danger of losing his life, John Nelson left for Plymouth, only to quarrel with his old associate, Benjamin Wills Newton. In December of that year he started a separate assembly, and 'Darbyism', as his sect was now called, spread to other places, including Bristol and London. His followers became known as Exclusives and later as Darbyites, when further fragmentations took place – individuals withdrawing from practices or the expression of beliefs which they believed to be wrong. The original group, however, known as the Bethseda or Open Brethren, continued to exist.

Thereafter he spoke and wrote prolifically. He visited Elbefeld in Germany in 1853 and spent the following year there, translating the New Testament into German. He preached all over Europe as well as writing two books, *The Sufferings of Christ* and *The Righteousness of God,* in 1858 and 1859, both so controversial that many of his followers deserted him.

Between 1859 and the late 1870s John Nelson Darby travelled to Canada, the United States, New Zealand and the West Indies to lecture and to preach. During those years he had been part of a team who translated the Old Testament into German, and had himself made a translation of it into French, which he completed in 1880. He also composed and published a number of hymns and wrote no fewer than thirty-two volumes of letters and tracts in his lifetime. One letter written to his brother Horatio at Leap in 1885 reveals his care and loving concern that his family should walk the path to salvation. He writes:

> I rejoice when you say pray God to make you more faithful to him. This is what we want for this only abides in its fruit and all

the rest perishes in the using. May you find the comfort and joy of living thoroughly out for the Lord.[21]

John Nelson Darby is sometimes regarded as quarrelsome but was in truth increasingly adamant about maintaining the purity of his vision, which consisted of absolute adherence to the word of God as exemplified in the Old and New Testaments, and following explicitly the teachings of Christ as the Son of God and the Saviour of mankind. Leaving aside the obstacle of human frailty, few would agree on exactly how to do either of these things in all circumstances.

In 1882 John Nelson died at Bournemouth, aged eighty-two, and his burial in the cemetery outside the town was attended by hundreds of his devoted followers, so many that a special train had to be provided to take the mourners back to London afterwards. There are still small gatherings of Brethren in many places, both in these islands and abroad, and the name of John Nelson Darby is still revered by Christians of all denominations, for he was a true Evangelical, spreading the gospel of Christianity round the world.

This deeply devout, learned and courageous man, whose fine Darby eyes burn with zeal in my favourite portrait of him, is, in my picture of a place and its people, like the touch of scarlet that Constable so often put into his predominantly green landscapes. John Nelson is the fiery contrast to those worthy pillars of the establishment, the other Darbys of Leap, bringing spiritual values to a scene that, albeit kindly and charitable, was essentially mundane. The Darbys had served King and Country for generations, getting on with the business of extracting a good yield from the land, fighting for the Crown when needed, administering justice and espousing good causes, all the while consolidating their position, enhancing their home, increasing their local prestige. John Nelson seems to have set little store by the gracious beauty of the home of his family, or by their worldly authority: he was a man with a mission that required a high degree of self-denial. There was in his message no room for compromise or pretension. He represents the Keep of the spirit; stout, foursquare, unadorned, the soul's bulwark against what Puritans such as he regarded as the vanities of materialism.

John Nelson Darby, my three times great-uncle, came from a family who were, in succeeding generations, far from puritanical, but his influence upon the locality lived on. My mother told of the meetings of the

21 See Appendix 3, where this letter appears in full.

local Brethren that still took place at Leap in her youth, and she suspected that the church services at Aghancon, already 'Low Church', became even more austere as a result of John Nelson's influence. She once made a beautiful cross of lilies from the hothouse at Leap to put on the Altar for Easter Sunday, but it was not allowed to be displayed. She never forgot her hurt and bewilderment. Grandfather himself respected the Brethren, though stoutly Church of Ireland himself.

The family members who were Brethren have a small plot surrounded by iron railings for their burial-ground, just outside the churchyard at Aghancon. All except John Nelson's brother Horatio, of whom more will be heard later. His grave is inside the churchyard, at the east end of the church, close by the north wall, well apart from the other Darby tombs. Was this a compromise?

William Henry Darby, John Nelson's eldest brother and himself a member of the Brethren, had succeeded his father John in 1834 and was married first, in about 1827, to Laura Caroline Curteis, with whom he had a son and a daughter. After Laura's death in 1847 William married, in 1848, Elizabeth Drought of King's County, and had no less than ten more: three sons and nine daughters in all. What with all those children, and the large assortment of servants required to keep the place going, the castle must have been full to overflowing.

It was during William's time at Leap that the Potato Famine raged in Ireland, from 1845 until 1851, reducing the population of the country from about eight million to just over six and a half million, not only from starvation and its subsequent effects but also from the emigration of the desperate to America on the infamous 'coffin ships' and, in lesser numbers, to north-west England and other parts of the Empire.

Until the onset of the Napoleonic wars, the Irish countryside had been for the most part used for grazing, but the British armies needed food and much of the land was turned over at that time to tillage for export of grain to England. When the wars ended, a situation had come about where the Irish themselves now relied almost exclusively on the potato as their staple food, and, with the land being put back to pasture use, very many labourers were forced out of work. These people and their large families had then to feed themselves on the potatoes that they could grow on the small patch of subdivided land that was allotted to them, eked out with produce from a cow that could be meagrely fed on whatever came to hand. In 1845 and the four succeeding years the entire potato crop of the island was ruined by blight; the animals died and the people had lost their sole source of sustenance. Some grain was still grown, but this was a 'cash crop' and, iniquitously, could not be used to feed the Irish population. Such help as was provided was too little, too late, and for the most part bungled by a goverment divided as to what should be done. So it fell to the landlords to do what they could from their own dwindling stocks of food and money. Some tried harder than others; the absentee landlords did not by and large acquit themselves very well. The people of the south and west fared the worst, for their land was not productive and in any event many of them were the descendants of the dispossessed and had no resources of their own. But this is not to say that almost unimaginable tragedy did not stalk the entire land.

Much has been written about this calamitous time, and opinions are many and divided about the the manner in which the disaster was handled by the English. It seems incredible to us today that the parent country of a colony could be so wrapped up in its own concerns that it allowed the situation in Ireland to assume the proportions of a major crisis. But such was the case, supported by a half-baked *laissez-faire* policy.

My grandmother, Milly Darby, wrote a remarkable book about the Potato Famine in the neighbourhood of Leap, called *The Hunger*, which came out in 1910.[22] For her material she went to the old tenants on the estate and to other neighbours to glean first-hand recollections, which she wove into a larger picture of the nation-wide catastrophe. The incidents related here deal with the experiences of all who were involved: the poorest people, the Quakers, the farmers, the professional people, the landlords and their families, and, not least, the ministers of both the Catholic and Protestant churches. Perhaps there were family memoirs, too, of how things were at Leap during those years, or letters to do with the crisis. She was, after all, writing of events that had taken place only just over forty years before her own arrival at Leap.

Milly, in her Introduction to *The Hunger*, writes:

> Life is too crowded to remember the events of the nineteenth in this busy twentieth century, or to pause and reflect how it was possible, within the recollection of living men, for two millions of fellow creatures to die of starvation, and the pestilence brought on by famine, not in the wilds of Africa or the plains of India, not in the remote regions of Asiatic Russia, but within eight hours journey of London, the richest city in the world, the heart of the

22 Published by Andrew Melrose, London.

Mother Country of the great Empire whose proudest boast it is that peace and prosperity are ensured under the Union Jack!

She goes on to give a vivid account of how the disaster came about, and describes a situation that is obviously drawn from life on the Leap estate:

An illustration of the peasants' want of knowledge regarding any foods but oatmeal stirabout and potatoes is found in a private record kept ... by a well-known land owner in the King's County, who spent the Famine Years living on his estate. In this journal it is mentioned that when he procured a shipload of rice and issued it to his people, universal dissatisfaction was expressed regarding the new food because 'it cranched under the teeth of the eaters'.

They had devoured it uncooked!

In the book itself, the causes are set out and the effects demonstrated in episodes from the lives of the people in the vicinity of Torrabegh Castle, obviously based on Leap. In reality, in spite of warnings from Lord Rosse, King's County displayed an initial local optimism; the threat of blight and famine was perceived to hang most heavily over distant places like Galway and, it was hoped, would keep away from this particular area of Ireland.[23] However, when disaster took hold, this was a district where much was attempted and achieved in the way of succour. The Darbys' role on their dependants' behalf was especially creditable, a point stressed by Milly Darby in this vividly written and well-researched account of the tragedy.

She gives a dramatic and knowledgeable account of the second onset of the blight in chapter 4, 'Fate's Thunderstorm Begins'. Cleary, the schoolmaster, leaves his house after a night of lashing wind and rain:

The distance between his cottage and the hedge-school was little over a hundred yards, but the mist was so thick that he wandered from the path before he reached the high road and found himself close to the garden where his patch of potatoes were planted.

The schoolmaster halted suddenly in his stride. An awful dread gripped at his heart, for a whiff of heavy odour had been wafted to him and filled his nostrils.

He stood thus for a full minute, the moisture congealing on the

23 'The Great Famine, Birr and District'. A lecture by historian Margaret Hogan, 1966.

> rough surface of his coat and in his hair; shut out by the fog from the whole universe, yet close knit to the millions of his fellow-countrymen by fearful foreboding and a suspicion he lacked the courage to investigate lest it should prove a fact.
>
> Cleary's forehead was damp with other dews than those of the enfolding mist, while he sniffed and sniffed again the heavy, rank, unmistakable smell. Once before he had smelt that tell-tale fore-runner of corruption, and he had no difficulty in recognising now the cause.
>
> He dried his horn-rimmed spectacles and replaced them on his nose, then stooped down to the ridges where his potatoes were growing and plucked a handful of the blossoms to examine them more closely.
>
> The stalks felt flaccid in his grasp, the beautiful flowers which twelve hours before had covered his garden with a purple carpet of imperial splendour were faded, and hung their heads in death. Below them, the erstwhile green leaves had grown sere and yellow and already showed a speckling of the hideous brown spots which were the outward sign of the 'new' disease that last season had destroyed the potatoes.
>
> 'The Blight! The potato rot! Merciful Heaven!' groaned Cleary. 'If it has come as bad this year as it was last season, what will be the end of us all? Mother of God! intercede for us! Sure the harvest that is before us 'ull be reaped be no mortal hand. An' the sheaves 'ull be men, an' women, and little childer – an' little childer, just as the old woman was saying last night.'
>
> He stood staring at the faded flowers, turning them over and over in his fingers while the probable consequences of this second visitation filled his mind with an overwhelming sense of disaster. The grim Reaper whose sickle was bared in the sunlight stood clearly before him. Too well the schoolmaster knew that the vapours charged with this sickly odour were heavy with death and decay – with death of more than the tubers already rotting and melting away in the ground at his feet.[24]

It is clear that William Henry Darby of Leap, who had inherited eleven years earlier, was among those landlords who did his utmost for the suffering people. When the workhouse at Birr was overflowing, he

24 *The Hunger*, pp. 71–2.

caused a fever shed, as these auxiliary houses were named, to be erected in the village at Leap, to give succour to those not only incapacitated by starvation but also, in some cases, a prey to the cholera epidemic which swept the area in the summer of 1849. His brother Horatio also worked tirelessly for the alleviation of suffering in the district: there is a letter extant dated 15 March 1846 in which Horatio requests the authorities, who were in receipt of a shipment of Indian corn, to allow him to purchase 'a few tons for the labourers in this district'.[25] Furthermore, *The King's County Chronicle* of 21 October 1846 carries the typescript of a long address to the Parsonstown Agricultural Society in which Horatio urges the members to practise self-denial, to give as much employment as possible and to pull together to make the best use of such strategems for survival as could be devised. His speech radiates Christian compassion and exhortation, as might be expected from the brother of John Nelson Darby, but is laced with practical propositions. Horatio was also an active as well as a financial supporter of the efforts of the third Earl of Rosse, direct descendant of Sir Laurence Parsons and the principal landlord of the Birr district. Lord Rosse was one of the few to foresee a failure of the potato crop and to attempt to avert the impact of it before it happened. He also worked hard to inform and rouse public opinion across the Irish Sea during the famine.[26]

It would not have been possible for Messrs Godkin and Walker to have got away with giving the following glowing account of William's later years at Leap in *The New Handbook of Ireland* had he not acquitted himself so well in the dreadful times that preceded these apparently contented years. The two authors evidently wrote it for the expanding tourist trade, and the part which refers to Leap, even allowing for sycophancy, paints a harmonious picture of the place in the days of my great-great-grandfather:

> Leap Castle, the seat of the Darby family, is a most interesting place.... It is difficult to imagine anything more charming than its situation. Approached by a short avenue from a road running along the side of a hill crowned with venerable trees, you enter by the ancient doorway. Passing through a spacious hall to the drawing room, you step out upon a terrace from which you see a vast plain lying far below, and stretching away towards the Slieve-Bloom mountains. In the distance this plain is covered with the

25 National Archives, RLFC/1/756/2/441/23.
26 Margaret Hogan. As above.

> dwellings of the tenantry of Mr. Darby, among the most contented and happy in the United Kingdom. They live in two storied slated houses, commodious and well kept, the farms clothed beautifully with timber trees, the large fields well sheltered with old hedgerows, and showing proof of a fair proportion of tillage and a judicious rotation of crops. The picture of peace and plenty was completed by numerous cattle and sheep grouped here and there on the rich pasture lands....
>
> Nothing can exceed their popularity with all classes and creeds in the country, the poor Catholics being most fervent of all in their praise. 'Ah,' said one of them, 'Mr Darby will not leave the poor man's children without milk. It must be our fault if we do not have a cow at the door.'
>
> Long ago, when few landlords were thinking about the condition of the agricultural labourer, or trying to make it better, the proprietor of Leap Castle erected for his workmen a number of slated houses, each with four large, well-aired rooms, a kitchen and parlour on the ground floor, and two bedrooms upstairs, with outside offices. He gives this house with grazing for a cow, a calf, and a donkey, and turf, for £4 a year, paid weekly, by a deduction from the wages. He pays 1s. a day in winter, 1s.3d. in summer. He lets none of his cottages except to his own workmen, and he expects that at least one able-bodied man from each house shall always be in his employment.[27]

Many of these houses, with their distinctive 'half-hipped' gables at each end of the roof, are still inhabited today and the widespread area over which they may be seen gives one an idea of the considerable size of the estates that, until the advent of the Land Laws, were presided over by the owners of Leap. William's grandmother, born Eleanor Lovett, would have been familiar with this type of roof, in Buckinghamshire, where she lived as a girl. She may well have been the influence, in her own days at Leap, which gave rise to the half-hipped gable becoming a hallmark of the estate domestic architecture so highly praised in the above account.

Life on the Leap estate may not have been so uniformly idyllic as the writers of *The New Handbook of Ireland* portray it, but it does seem that William Henry Darby's provision of the houses and conditions

27 pp. 242–4.

described there was unusual for the times. This is borne out by the historian Margaret Hogan. In her lecture to the local History Seminar in Birr in 1966 she mentions a commission of inquiry set up by the British government into the state of poverty in the locality in the first half of the nineteenth century, in which it was reported that the houses of the poor were:

> of the worst materials, with clay walls roofed with branches or covered with rushes or sods... Labourers were generally allowed the grass for a cow by their employers and sometimes a plot to sow potatoes, and their principal food was potatoes, salt and a little milk... Three stones of potatoes would be required to provide three meals a day for a family with three or four children.[28]

The Leap employees seem to have enjoyed a much less deprived existence, indeed the period after the famine appears to have been the heyday of Leap's fortunes. If the above account is to be believed, it was a time when the estate was a happy place with a popular landlord. However, the tide had started to turn against the Protestant Ascendancy as early as the 1840s, with the advent of a revived sense of Irishness. It began among the middle classes, and spread to the poorer country tenantry when John Mitchel,[29] a young social reformer, urged the peasantry to revolt against the landlords and fight for the establishment of independence for Ireland. If the tenants at Leap remained as content as we are led to believe, it says a great deal for William Henry Darby as a landlord.

In 1850 Charles Gavin Duffy, the editor of a prestigious Dublin journal, *The Nation*, founded the Tenants' Rights League, which advocated fair rents and the tenant's right to sell his interest at a price that took into account any improvements to the property that he had made. This and other long-awaited reforms came to nothing, however, and it was not until 1870 that Gladstone's first Land Act (hated by the landlords) led to recognition of the rights of tenants. This Act aimed at improving the tenant's lot, making it compulsory for landlords to compensate tenants for dismissal, or eviction for other reasons, and possible for the latter to purchase the land they occupied. In 1879 the Irish National Land League was founded, which eroded further the landlords' supremacy over their territories, and from then onwards a campaign of

28 'The Great Famine, Birr and District'. Lecture by Margaret Hogan, 1966.
29 1815–75.

overt militancy against landlordism itself was waged with growing intensity. For the likes of the Darbys, this was the beginning of the end.

William Henry Darby, 'wonderfully hale and hearty', according to the writers of *The New Handbook of Ireland,* lived on until 1880, when he was nearly eighty-nine years old. The eldest son, Jonathan, married to his mother's cousin, Caroline Curteis, had predeceased him in 1872 aged just forty-five, and had been for some unknown reason disinherited. Why should a father inflict such shame on a young man of apparently exemplary character, a barrister, a justice of the peace from 1858, and evidently held in affection and respect by the local people?[30] It seems that William Henry Darby was not all that benevolent after all, but we must not discount the possibility that the father simply did not think his son physically fit enough to hold down the job of landlord. In the event, the property passed to William's grandson, Jonathan Charles Darby, the eldest surviving son of his father, without a painful situation arising between parent and child.

What of this Jonathan, my grandfather? There are only the barest of biographical facts to go on. Jonathan Charles Darby was born on 28 April 1855 at Ashley Place, Westminster, the second son of his father, his elder brother having died in infancy. Still a schoolboy at Blackheath College when his father died, Jonathan went up to Lincoln College, Oxford, in 1874, where he read Law and distinguished himself as an athlete. Thereafter, he prepared himself seriously for the life of an influential landlord, going straight from Oxford to British Columbia to learn forestry and farming, and returning there several times after he came into his property. Sadly, no early photographs of my grandfather have come to light, but he was said to have been very handsome as a young man.

Jonathan became the owner of the Leap estate, comprising 4,637 acres in the King's County (as well as some 207 acres in Worcestershire)[31] at a time when landlords in Ireland were having an increasingly difficult job keeping their heads above water. To make matters worse, he inherited considerable debts, and was obliged to sell precious land in order to pay them.[32] An added difficulty was his background. Although he would have spent his early childhood in the vicinity of Leap, since his father served that community, my grandfather, as we

30 See Appendix 5.
31 *The Great Landowners of Great Britain and Ireland*, compiled by John Bateman in 1876 and reprinted by Leicester University Press in 1971.
32 Land Commission Record No. S 367.

have seen, was educated exclusively in England. Thereafter he trained and worked overseas, with brief respites at his widowed mother's London home or with his cousins at Marklye in Sussex (according to his daughter Patricia). He can have had little knowledge of the way things worked in Ireland, nor would he have any idea of how to get on with his tenants, to whom he would have been a comparative stranger.

Nevertheless, things began promisingly for the new landlord, as evidenced by an article in *The Kings County Chronicle* of 22 July 1880 entitled REJOICINGS AT LEAP CASTLE, which describes the welcome given to 'Mr. Darby, his mother, and family, on the occasion of their taking possession and coming to reside in Leap Castle.' An immense bonfire blazed, and 'the entire tenantry on the Leap Castle estate attended, anxious to offer to their young landlord... the most cordial of welcomes'. A fiddler played for the dancing, and 'refreshments were abundantly provided'. Declarations of loyalty and goodwill were exchanged, and published on another page.[33] In the same newspaper, dated 7 January 1886, the following account provides a colourful vignette of more festivities at Leap. Entitled CHRISTMAS TREE AT LEAP CASTLE, the article ran as follows:

> The annual Christmas Tree and Children's Fete was held on the evening of New Year's Day in the Great Hall of Leap Castle. The sight, as one entered, was magnificent, the Hall, which is a sight in itself at any time, being very tastefully decorated with wreaths of evergreens, suspended from the surrounding gallery, whilst all around were devices wrought 'with cunning workmanship' by Miss Darby and many assistants, the motto most prominent being 'God bless our Queen and Country', the whole being brilliantly lighted with Chinese lanterns and myriads of wax tapers fastened to the Tree which was, of course, the centre of attention. After the children had had a hearty repast, various games were indulged in, everyone being in the best of humour. The Tree, next, was soon stripped, and its manifold 'fruits' distributed amongst the children, whose thanks and those of their parents were tendered to Miss Darby by Mr. Theophilous Wallace, and a 'Hip, hip, hurrah' ... from one hundred and fifty little throats made the vaulted roof of Old Leap Castle ring and ring again. Cheers were given for Mr. Darby, who, although he was four thousand miles away had not

33 See Appendix 5.

> at this festive season forgotten the juveniles on his estates, as he had sent two barrels of apples, rich and ripe, for the occasion from the 'Golden West'... The singing of the 'National Anthem' brought this very enjoyable evening to a close.

This charming picture of Anglo-Irish paternalism is the more poignant on account of the writing already so clearly on the wall. How heartfelt were those cheers amongst the parents? Hard to guess, but a further excerpt from this same newspaper, dated 7 January 1886, suggests that Jonathan was still very much liked. Under the heading of RETURN OF MR. DARBY, the announcement reads:

> After a tour of some months through Canada and the United States, in the former of which he has a leading property,[34] J. C. Darby Esq. J.P. has returned to his Irish Seat at Leap Castle, Roscrea. This popular young gentleman's return is hailed with the sincerest joy by his numerous Yeomen, the honestest tenantry on his estate, who, it is only justice to say, are such a credit to Ireland that if all were like them, there would be little heard of the galvanised cry about Home Rule.

With hindsight, it is obvious that the proprietors *of The King's County Chronicle* were whistling in the dark. It seems probable, however, that the Leap tenants felt genuinely loyal, even affectionate, towards their landlord and his family while at the same time fulminating with the desire for Home Rule.

In 1882, soon after he succeeded, Jonathan was made High Sheriff of the county, and the following year he became the Vice President of the Birr division of the Unionist Association. He is said to have been 'non-political', which I take to mean that he knew what he stood for but was no agitator. However, he was the master of the local lodge of the Orange Institution at Aghancon, and was, together with the Earl of Rosse, an area representative on the Grand Lodge of Ireland. The Orange order was, as now, a stoutly Protestant and Anglophile institution, formed in 1795 and named after William of Orange: hardly non-political! A member of the Board of Guardians of the Orphans' Association, my grandfather subsequently became Deputy Lord Lieutenant of the county and was serving the community in that capacity at the time of the burning of Leap. He was also on the Grand Jury Panel,

34 Unidentified.

as were all the most prominent landowners of each county, and served as a justice of the peace from 1882 until his enforced flight from the vicinity. A picture emerges of a typical landlord of his standing and background, stoutly loyal to the Crown and acting responsibly and, let it be remembered, voluntarily, on its behalf.

What was Jonathan like, as a young and middle aged-man? Despite the favourable references to him in the local press in his early days as landlord, he has come down to us as a veritable ogre, on account of his wife Milly's letters and of many stories of varying authenticity: instances of his choleric disposition, ranging from impatience and intolerance to fits of uncontrollable and terrifying rage. His perceived shortcomings lead one to suspect that he would have been unlikely to approach his role of landlord in a spirit of humility. He was an authoritarian through and through, but this does not make him a monster. I see him rather as a man who came into his inheritance at a time when its days were numbered, and he fought for survival in the only way he knew.

Following the founding of the Irish National Land League, a further Act in 1881, just after my grandfather inherited Leap, instituted the Land Commission. This gave tenants the right to seek reduction of their rents and made loans of up to three-quarters of the purchase price to those who wanted to own their holdings. Later Acts eroded still further the power of the landlords, eventually necessitating the sale of many large estates to the government, who sold them on, piecemeal, to the tenants, who could now pay the whole sum by easy instalments. All this happened gradually during and after my grandparents' occupation of Leap. Although, as we have observed, land had had to be sold when Jonathan first inherited the place, it is an indication of the estate's former size that it still comprised well over 3,000 acres at the time of the burning. My grandfather was much more fortunate in this respect than many other landowners. However, Jonathan was a gentleman farmer with a number of tenants, not a titled magnate with substantial property elsewhere to offset his losses. With no independent income, he must have been in a permanent state of anxiety, which cannot have improved his temper. Indeed, it is not impossible that it was the difficulties of his position that caused Jonathan to become the tyrannical person recalled by so many. More about this will emerge in a later chapter.

Although he had inherited the Leap estate in 1880, it was not until 1889 that my grandfather wooed and won my grandmother, Mildred

Dill, who had all the attributes, on the face of it, of the perfect wife for a landed gentleman determined to survive. Milly turned out to be someone more interesting than just that. She was a powerful person in her own right – something her husband had not bargained for.

6
Milly

PART ONE: EARLY LIFE

Mildred Henrietta Gordon Dill, or Milly as she was known to her family and friends, was born on March 13th, 1869, the youngest of six children. Her father, Dr Richard Gordon Dill, was a respected physician practising in Brighton. As a young man he had served as a medical officer in China with General Gordon, who was a cousin by marriage, before returning to England to inherit the Brighton practice from his Uncle John, who had been a surgeon in the old East India Company Navy. In 1856 Richard married Augusta Caroline, known as Molly, the beautiful daughter of General Sir Charles Wale KCB, who, having spent the early part of her married life having children (though her achievement of a mere half-dozen was nothing compared with that of her mother, who had had fifteen), reputedly passed the rest of her days reclining elegantly on a sofa until she died in 1925 aged 102. In her photographs, however, she has such a wise, alert and intelligent face that it is difficult to imagine her idle in all respects.

Dr Dill, who is said to have been both handsome and charming as well as successful in his profession, prospered sufficiently to buy a piece of land in the then village of Burgess Hill, outside Brighton, where he built a splendid mansion, Birchwood, to house his growing family. It was not all that far from the Darbys' house at Marklye. To us, Birchwood looks enormous for a doctor's residence, but in Victorian eyes it would have been seen as a suitable, solid home for people of the Dills' position in society. A couple of surviving snapshots reveal an interior serviceable rather than opulent, with no sofa in evidence upon which one could hope to recline in any comfort. Perhaps Molly had a boudoir where stuffed horsehair and wickerwork gave place to plushy upholstery. She spent her early years in accommodation befitting a general's rank while her father was a serving soldier, and she subsequently lived at Little Shelford Hall, Cambridgeshire, where he inherited an estate, so she may well have had rather grander ideas than the Dills. Grand ideas are apt to stick, and this was certainly so amongst the younger members of the family and their offspring, who mostly continued to live in the style to which they had become accustomed, whether it could be afforded or not. What seemed to their spouses to be luxuries were regarded as necessities, and money, if not actually earned or inherited in sufficient quantities to provide them, had to be 'found', and was, like mushrooms, generally to be had if you knew where to look. (Milly's eldest daughter – my mother – was an old hand at this game.)

The Dills were of Anglo-Irish Plantation stock; that is to say they were granted land in Ulster under James I, in exchange for which they had to meet stringent obligations similar to those undertaken by the Darbys, further south, already described in chapter 2. In addition, the Ulster settlers were ordered to build defences round their newly acquired property. They also had to bring in ten Protestant families from either England or Scotland for each 1,000 acres of their land, and to oversee the creation of viable and productive farming units on what had hitherto been virtually uncultivated areas of the north west. Thus, at one stroke, two objectives were achieved: a large influx of Protestants and the implementation of an intensive agricultural project.

The first Dill to feature in the pages of *Burke's Irish Family Records* is one John Dill of Tullynadel, Donegal, who was living in 1665. His son, David, married Catherine Sheridan of Drogeda; 'a lady of great pride and courage, who reputedly killed the last wolf in Ireland', says Burke. An interesting early strand in the DNA, which seems to have prevailed. The family continued to be landowners in that area until around the turn of the nineteenth century when Springfield, the family home, was pulled down. Richard Dill would not have inherited, being a younger son of a younger son, the Revd Richard Dill of Ballykelly, so it is not surprising that he availed himself of the opportunity to set up home and a medical practice, at his uncle's behest, at 19, Regency Square, in fashionable Brighton.

Of the six Dill children, Milly was the youngest by four years. By good fortune, a lively and perspicacious account of life at Birchwood in her time and in the next generation is given by George Montague Stevens in his delightful memoir, *Rambling through the 1880s and Beyond.*[1] George was the son of Milly's elder sister Helen. She had married Monty Stevens, a devastatingly attractive Cambridge University friend of her brothers who went cattle ranching in New Mexico. George tells us that John Dill, the eldest son, became a fine doctor, as

1 Privately printed.

did the next brother in line, Bob, who enlisted in the Army as a captain in the Medical Corps and was killed in a skirmish with tribesmen in India. George's other two uncles, Richard and George, trained as barristers, but Richard, doted on by his mother, and possessed of a brilliant legal brain, became an alcoholic and lived mostly at home until the 1914 war, when he joined a theatrical group to entertain troops in the trenches and died of wounds in 1918, having been hit by a mortar bomb.

Helen, senior to Milly by four years, had a beautiful contralto voice and studied music in London during the early 1880s, while Milly continued her education into her late teens, probably at some institution in Brighton, having decided to become a writer. George Stevens says that she attended a university, but there is no evidence of this, and indeed it is most improbable: her parents were Plymouth Brethren and would never have allowed it. Singing was a womanly accomplishment, learning was not. However, Milly did manage to furnish herself with quite a wide knowledge of history, literature, languages and the classics, as her books testify, and, naturally, she knew her Bible. Since she had set her heart on a literary career, it seems surprising that she should have married so young (she was twenty), unless it was to some extent because this was what her parents considered the proper destiny for any woman, however gifted. Perhaps she just fell in love. (Jonathan, like many of his descendants, had beautiful hands and legs, and very fine eyes.) My instinct is that she needed to escape from the restraints of the parental home and was seduced by the prospect of marrying Jonathan and becoming the chatelaine of Leap. That she was wilful, tempestuous and a bit of a firebrand by nature is hinted at in a letter from Jonathan to his mother-in-law, written on the day after their wedding, and borne out by Milly's resentful, anguished reaction to the subsequent frustrations and privations of her married life. Jonathan's letter, dated 9 November 1889, thanks Molly for 'all the trouble you have taken about our affairs and this function at B. Wood', and continues: 'I only hope you will lend an eye to see that Milly's things are safely packed for her, otherwise there will be a glorious smash and a vast chaos of broken crockery, as we all say at home'. Prophetic words, as we shall see. Much later, on 26 June 1909, he writes again to Molly, while his wife is absent from home, 'I hear Milly is on the rampage again.' Her bursts of fury seem to have been taken quite for granted which no doubt increased the mounting sense of frustration which is so vividly revealed in the few of her letters that survive.

Diana, my mother, maintained that before Milly became engaged, she suddenly left home to join the Salvation Army. Some credence is given to this by a letter written in the early Thirties to her daughter Patricia,[2] as well as in 'Via Dolorosa' and others of her published stories. It is not hard to envisage the consternation this defection would have caused within the Dill family who, however evangelically inclined, would have felt that it threatened their respectability. However, it is clear from her writings that Milly at some point before her marriage was engaged in work among London's poor. Her observations, though shot through with compassion for the victims, are mischievously ironic and shrewd in their depictions of the mixed motives of the do-gooders, and could only have been drawn from experience.

Milly was not strikingly beautiful, but pictures of her at around the time of her marriage to Jonathan reveal a neatly proportioned, elegant girl whose intelligence shines out, giving an edge to her prettiness. It is not a serene countenance, even if allowance is made for the contrived, unsmiling pose required by Victorian convention. She looks serious, thoughtful and every inch a lady of quality, upon whose head an academic cap would have sat as easily as the ornate confections of the era. With a prosperous background and considerable personality and grace, the younger Miss Dill was clearly a catch. Caroline Darby, in a letter to Molly Dill at the time of her son's engagement to Milly, writes as follows:

> Dearest Mrs. Dill,
>
> Yes, I am equally glad to have dearest Milly for a belle-fille. I have often thought it possible, and lately probable. I do not think there is any girl I love better than Milly.

A widow and in poor health, Caroline Darby must have been relieved as well as delighted at her son's choice of a bride. He was thirty-five years old so this was an appropriate time for him to take a wife. The future looked bright; set fair for the continuation of the Darbys of Leap Castle within the solid, domestic Victorian tradition.

2 'When I got to New York I found … a letter from Eva Booth to ask me to go and dine with her at the S.A. Headquarters. This I did and VERY pleased we both were to meet again.' General Evangeline Booth (b. 1864) was the daughter of General William Booth, celebrated founder of the Salvation Army, and the subject of a wonderful poem by Vachel Lindsay: 'General William Booth Enters into Heaven'. See *The Faber Book of Modern Verse*, p. 151.

PART TWO: MARRIED MILLY

Milly and Jonathan were married from Birchwood on 7 November 1889. There is a charming description of the homecoming after their honeymoon in the *Midland Tribune* of the following day, under the heading 'Rejoicings at Leap Castle'. The following is an extract from that account:

> The hoary, monumental gateway of the Castle was transformed into a noble triumphal arch, with the word 'Welcome'. Chinese lanterns were used with picturesque effect and a huge bonfire of turf, tar barrels and bogwood was lit up at dusk, throwing the ancient Castle and its surroundings into bold effect. Down the drive hundreds of dancing jet flames showed a thousand beauties of light and shade, each intermingling with the other and casting a fairy like charm over the whole scene. The noble old hall was gaily festooned with Union Jacks and flags, conspicuous among them being the flag of the Leap Independents... It was a picturesque scene viewed from the terrace. The extensive sweeping lawn, thickly dotted with oak, ash, sycamore and beech, with the noble background of the mountains. Over the hall door hung the Irish motto *Caed Milte Failthe*, while the numerous lights of the castle shone out brilliantly.
>
> On each window were placed horse shoes to bring good luck and to keep away ghosts, for Leap Castle has hosts of traditions, even of ghosts. Arriving at the foot of the hill, the carriage of Mr. Darby and his bride was drawn home by the cheering tenantry, while a band of musicians gave full merriment to the scene, and thus were the bride and bridegroom drawn to the threshold of their home, one of the oldest in Hibernia. Mr. Darby stood up in his carriage and said 'On behalf of Mrs. Darby and myself, I heartily thank you all. When you see Mrs Darby in the morning you will say I have not done wrong'. The happy couple entered the castle when suddenly the bride came back, and with a slight quiver of excitement in her voice, but in clear tones said, 'Friends, on this occasion I do not want my husband to have all the talk to himself. Though it is very hard for me to leave my happy home, yet with the hearty, warm-felt Irish reception I have received, it comes much easier on me [sic]. I trust that in a few days I shall personally get to know you all'. Ringing cheers resounded to the little

> speech, intermingled with reverent words of approbation, such as 'You're a whole woman, that you are and no mistake' while several old women pensioners knelt by the steps and said 'God bless the gran' weeny crather.' The large assembly then returned to the fire 'tripping the light fantastic toe', in the blaze, presenting the most fantastic and weird picture. At eight o'clock Mr. and Mrs. Darby presented themselves and joined gaily in the proceedings for a short time… [Here follows a description of Presentations.]
>
> The real enjoyment then commenced. The Waltz and Polka and the Irish jig were kept up in that weird open air ballroom in the glare of the leaping flames into the early hours of the morning. In the witching maze of the dance gaiety banished all remembrance of the ghostly legends that haunted the site of long past wonder. Even the screech of the owl was unheeded, until the breaking day reminded them that weary feet must rest, whereupon all departed, wishing long life and happiness to the newly wedded pair.

This eyewitness account presents a vivid picture of the hopes and joys, however ephemeral, felt by the people of Leap at this start of a new phase of life. Was Jonathan annoyed or proud when his wife slipped back onto the terrace to have her own say? This was no shrinking violet of a bride. I cannot imagine that he suggested it. It is typical of the Milly we are beginning to discover; a pointer of the way things would go.

It would be interesting to know where 'the happy couple' spent their honeymoon, in the unromantic and chilly month of November, before settling into Leap as man and wife, and if there were already flies discernible in the honey. Things certainly began to go amiss before long. George Montague Stevens, living in America, relates in his memoirs that Richard Dill, the delightful alcoholic mother's pet of the family, described Milly's marriage as follows:

> My sister Milly married a wealthy Irishman and has lived married to the Establishment and is raising a nice family almost by herself. Her husband is too busy living by the Establishment which believes in working the Irish peasants, who by cheap labor enable him to live the life of Riley, a great deal of his time being spent in Paris. When revenues are low from his estate in Ireland he is always able to raise the assessment of taxes to be

paid by the peasants if they wish to continue farming his very rich estate.

This slant on Milly and Jonathan's marriage can only have come from Milly's conversations and correspondence with her sister Helen Stevens, bringing up her own family in New Mexico. It has the ring of her voice uplifted in complaint. (The reference to the life of Riley is an anachronism which was unintentionally used by George Stevens at a time when it was a *façon de parler.)*

While sympathising with the young Mrs Darby's predicament, perhaps one should regard this account as only one side of the story. All the same, it must bear some semblance to the truth. The term 'married to the Establishment' is interesting. Had the naturally rebellious Milly decided that it would be wise for her to live in that safe, conventional section of society? Many people, distrusting the vehemence of their own feelings, have chosen to marry into a world of constrictions where their impulses will be harnessed, usually with disastrous consequences to both parties. And let us not forget Jonathan's undoubted attractiveness, nor the lure of Leap itself. Neither of them, I feel sure, had had any idea of what each was letting the other in for when they exchanged their marriage vows.

With Milly constantly in mind on my recent trip to Leap, I was unexpectedly moved to tears by the small, ugly plaque on the wall of the little church at Aghancon, to the right of the altar. 'In loving memory', it reads, 'of Jonathan Richard, Son of J. C. Darby of Leap Castle. Died 30th April 1892. Aged four weeks.' Underneath is the text 'I shall go to Him'. Jonathan's son. No mention of Milly, in accordance with contemporary convention. He was hers for just four weeks. Were they happy weeks? Did he die suddenly? Or were they weeks of anguish as a sickly baby sank into death? We shall never know. There is, however, an account of the birth and death of a premature child in Milly's novel *Anthropoid Apes*, of 1909, which combines acute observation and the use of deliberately crass words in a description given with almost sinister detachment. These pages are intended to shock, and they do. Milly is watching, not feeling. It seems that she has, to use a modern phrase, been there, and devised her own way of dealing with the pain:

> It was an old, odd looking infant, its little face, hardly larger than a fair-sized salt cellar, lined and seamed in every direction. Its eyelids were tight shut, and the eyeballs seemed shrunken into its head; its ears, bat-like in their size and out of all proportion, stood out from the bare skull with grotesque prominence, and one tiny

> wrist like the plucked leg of a barnyard fowl, with a minute, tightly clenched fist, showed from beneath the swathing of cotton wool. But to Susan her child was the most beautiful object in the world.

The use of the word 'object' squashes any possible upsurge of sentimentality in the reader.

Unless his arrival was premature, little Jonathan Richard was not conceived until some seventeen months after Jonathan and Milly's marriage. Since Jonathan would have been anxious to start a family, preferably with a son and heir, it is quite possible that Milly had already had a miscarriage before her firstborn son. This would have added to her sense of frustration, failure and sorrow. She had allied herself with this family, assumed to be of royal Irish blood and inhabiting a seat of supposedly immense age, so the presentation of a male child to her lineage-conscious husband would have been her first duty – and indeed inclination. She was, after all, from an old Anglo-Irish Plantation family herself, a worthy contributor to the Darby blood line. Her inherently ironic attitude to most things did not, I am sure, extend at this stage to her marital duty and position in Society. Milly was expected to produce a boy. She had done so, and he had died. I believe that this event may have been one with which Milly never came to terms.

Seventeen months later, on 7 August 1893, my mother was born at Leap. Milly treated the aptly named Diana[3] as a boy from the word go, cutting her hair short and dressing her in boy's clothes. Later, she told her that she was to become a surgeon when she grew up, which caused her sister Cissie, two years younger, all curls and frills and simpers in her photographs, to inquire, 'Please mother, can I be just a plain lady?' When Horatio came along in 1898, Diana recalled that she was still dressed in tweed knickerbockers, and she continued to have cropped hair until she and Cissie were sent away in their teens to be educated in England, so completely had her mother transferred her lost son's identity onto her eldest daughter. In this situation it is impossible to disentangle cause from effect. Let it just be said that Diana, tall, strong and vigorous, had a happy childhood shooting, fishing, hunting and playing at boys' games with her young male cousins and neighbours and that Horatio, a short-sighted and to judge from his photographs gentle, rather fragile child, seems almost like the second son of the Darbys of Leap. He was always known as Boysie by the family; a form of

3 Diana (Artemis) was the Greek goddess of hunting.

endearment current at the time for a cherished son. That Uncle Boysie grew into a handsome and brave adult, full of character and much loved and respected by his wife and three sons, indicates that he came unscathed through this, to us, odd childhood. Perhaps his father was not party to his mother's fantasy about Diana.

In 1904 Milly gave birth to their fifth and final child, Florence Patricia O'Carroll, known for years as 'Flops'. Like all her siblings, she had the Darby eyes, but was in other respects much more similar in appearance to her mother's side of the family. Had Milly and Jonathan hoped for another son? My guess is that they had. Although she would certainly have been welcomed and loved from the start, it seems that she was aware, albeit semi-consciously, that she was a little apart from the others, who treated her, she said later, as a cross between a pet and a nuisance, so that she lacked for life the self-confidence that was so marked a feature of her sisters' characters. Anyone who arrived in this world as a girl when a boy was wanted will know what I speak of. Observe her in the family group at Birchwood, taken on Richard and Molly's Golden Wedding day in 1907: grave, a little apprehensive, rather on the edge of the scene. Today, someone would have been holding her hand.

No one knows when Jonathan and Milly's marriage began to run into difficulties. If George Stevens's report on Jonathan's dalliance in Paris is to be believed, it was quite early on, and this sounds like an immature man's escape from a difficult domestic situation in which Milly may have been absorbed in her children and her writing, and less subservient than her husband would have liked. It is obvious, too, that she was the cleverer of the two, and Jonathan would have found that infuriating. Indeed, the towering rages to which he was prone were already a part of my mother's recollections when she was quite small. They were all terrified of their father as children, and even later on he was still able to reduce his family to near-paralysis by his violence. One Christmas Day during the Great War he got up from the dining table at Leap to carve the turkey and found that the parlourmaid had inadvertently put the cold plates intended for a ham on the sideboard in front of the bird, and the hot ones beside the ham. With a bellow of fury, my grandfather hurled both lots of plates onto the floor, one by one, as the family sat in horrified silence. Returning to his place at the head of the table, he ordered fresh plates to be brought. No one who was present on that extraordinary occasion ever forgot it.

Milly's writing, I recall being told, annoyed Jonathan exceedingly from early on in their marriage. At the same time it must have been, for her, a saving grace, an escape from the tensions in the house and an essential outlet for her creative energy.

In 1898, just over a hundred years ago, my grandmother had a story published in a collection entitled *Under One Cover*. She wrote, it will be recalled, under the pen name of Andrew Merry, and such was the virility of her style and the carefully cultivated male viewpoint of all her writing (including passages of sly sentimentality about pretty women) that her secret remained undiscovered by the world at large for some years. This story, 'An April Fool', some sixty pages long and written with an eye to the middlebrow market, is professionally constructed, full of shrewd detail and masterly in its clear, incisive style. Understandably, it is also full of the prejudices of the day – racism and snobbery in particular – but aside from that, it gives a detailed picture of several aspects of contemporary life in England and Ireland, draws lively and convincing pictures of a variety of characters, and carries one along, often very amusingly, at a good pace. Milly's ear for dialogue is excellent, bringing to life the widely different characters that people her work. (It only becomes tedious when, in her later output, she gives us page after page of talk in the Irish country idiom of the day, which, however colourful, tires the reader.)

Milly was never a 'girly' girl. She rode well to hounds, was a fine shot and realised early on that it was a man's world that she inhabited. She is said to have been already a professional writer at the time of her marriage, though we have no record of her early work, and it is tempting to surmise that what originally fascinated Jonathan Darby was exactly what later infuriated him. In marrying a young woman of spirit, it can never have occurred to him that he would not exercise the domination over her that he seems later to have required of all members of his family. Had his wife been submissive by nature, Jonathan might not have become so domineering; stronger men than he have resorted to macho tactics when confronted with what they did not understand and could not control. Perhaps there is a metaphor here for England's treatment of the Irish.

By 1909 'Andrew Merry' had published several more short stories and three novels, two of them about Ireland, often based on life at Leap. The latter are as amusing as they are informative, written with a real respect for and understanding of the poorer people of the vicinity. She pokes gentle fun at the rogues of all walks of life, and, when her subject matter takes her further afield, at the pretensions of the newly rich, the weaknesses of the privileged and the hypocrisies of some of the philanthropists. It is not difficult to spot the autobiographical details that crop up constantly in thin disguise. Milly wrote about what she knew, and therein lies her strength. In her fourth and final novel, however, my grandmother writes with a depth of feeling and understanding that puts it in a different category. This book, *The Hunger*, already quoted in the previous chapter, gives the reader a vivid and heartrending series of insights into the sufferings of the people of central Ireland during the Potato Famine. It has a ring of authenticity about it that gives it real merit.

Now Milly was dealt a terrible blow. She was forbidden by her husband to write any more novels or stories, ostensibly on account of some sensational 'purple passion' tales that she is said to have written for one of the popular newspapers. Jonathan was, to quote my cousin John Minchin, 'wild with rage'. The effect on my grandmother can scarcely be imagined; she was only forty years old and had been a published writer for at least eleven years.

Since mine is a story centred on Leap, it is not the place to enlarge on the merits of my grandmother's novels and stories.[4] Suffice it to say that they were well received at the time of their publication and deserve to be read both as a commentary on their time and as works of art.[5] How might her literary skills have developed had she not been prevented from continuing her writing career? I doubt if Milly would ever have reached the first rank of contemporary novelists. For all her talent and expertise, she seems to have lacked the quality of vision, the capacity to lift a story onto the level of universal truth which is the hallmark of writing of the highest order, but I have no doubt that she would have continued to produce entertaining, informative work that would have consolidated her place in Irish literary history.

In 1910 Milly had a serious accident. When out driving her beloved trotting ponies she was tipped out of the carriage onto her head. She was unconscious for three weeks and was never quite the same afterwards, convinced that her ponies had been terrified by a spectre invisible to her. Her nerves were permanently affected and she became a chain-smoker. By this time she and Jonathan were on distant if not

4 Milly's published work includes: *An April Fool* (1898) *The Naked Truth* (1900), *The Green Country* (1902), *Paddy Risky* (1903), *Anthropoid Apes* (1909), *The Hunger* (1910), all published in London.

5 Stephen Brown, S.J., *Ireland in Fiction: A Guide to Irish Novels, Tales, Romances and Folklore*, vol. 1 (Irish University Press, Shannon, 1969), p. 211. 'Her writings are noted for their impartial standpoint as regards Irish questions, and for their virile style. Never in the criticism of her literary work has it been suggested that the pen-name hid a woman.'

actually hostile terms, but convention decreed that they should put a good face on their marriage.

To begin to appreciate Milly's complex nature and the effect she had on her children, one must see her in the context of her times, her upbringing and her social position. The concept of duty, so vital in my grandmother's time, prevailed above all. The 'stern daughter of the voice of God', of whom Wordsworth speaks in his 'Ode to Duty', was disregarded at one's peril, and in Milly's case there was the added spur of an uncompromising religious background, one in which resignation in adversity was paramount. To her, the new science of psychology was dangerous and corrupting. In her story 'An April Fool', Milly describes Jonathan Campbell, the parson, as follows: '... he was never the prey of conflicting doubts and fears, or of the morbid introspection that is the curse of the age'.[6] Milly despised that. I cannot imagine that she would have had any time for Freud, Jung or any of their contemporaries in that field. In her book, you made your bed and thereafter you had, with God's help, to lie on it.

I have heard tell from more than one source that after her accident Milly was from time to time to be seen driving her pony and trap at a gallop around Birr, her hair flying in the wind, her dress scanty and in a state of disarray. I do not think that this was an instance of her defying convention; that would have been out of character. It seems more likely that the story indicates the anguish and frustration she endured at the hands of her husband while in a state of mental fragility. Today's woman in the same situation might well get in the car, slam the door and drive furiously until she felt sane again.

Milly, as had been evident in her youth, was by nature a rebel. Had her ethical principles and social mores permitted it, she could have been a revolutionary. In a letter (of March 1917) to Sydney Carroll, she writes: 'Alas, it has never been my priviledge [*sic*] to meet those of the "Artistic" Militant Patriots of our native country you name.' There speaks a woman on the outside, looking in. Yet – within the milieu that she perforce inhabited – she was ahead of her times, with a social conscience far more developed than that of the prosperous do-gooders she mocks so mischievously in her books. Her capacity for indignation, being held in check, never fired changes for the better, but found such outlet as it could within the conventional bounds of her novels, until she was forbidden to write any more. Milly had all the instincts of a

6 p. 37.

social reformer, but, being unable to escape her background, seems to have become caught up in the web of her own sufferings. These she concealed from the world at large behind the façade of a rather mannish-looking gentlewoman in a haze of smoke from the Turkish cigarettes which remorselessly succeeded each other in her elegant tortoiseshell holder, and eventually killed her.

Was she embittered? Perhaps inevitably so, in view of her enforced cessation from writing and her husband's resentment and ill-treatment of her. Moreover, not one of her children shared her tastes or measured up to her intellect. She tried to get the girls educated at her cousin Olive Willis's new school, Downe House, in Kent, but Jonathan did not hold with educating women, and only permitted them to go, on a far from regular basis, to a day-school in Brighton, living with Milly's parents at Burgess Hill. This he grudgingly allowed, when governesses could no longer control them and their high spirits looked like landing them in serious trouble. There was the episode of the dog-cart, overturned to discover if the incumbent of the unenviable post of governess to the young Darbys wore a wig; and numerous tales exist of mice, toads and other livestock being planted in the poor woman's bed. My mother maintained that they learned much in the farms and stables, practically nothing in the schoolroom. Milly seems eventually to have given up the struggle to get her two elder daughters any regular schooling, while Horatio, of course, ran the gamut of preparatory and public schools in England. Flops, much loved, but so inconvenient an afterthought, was eventually sent to boarding school in England in spite of her father's objections, since no one seemed to know what else to do with her. (She preferred to be known as Patricia, which I shall call her from now on.)

Milly's sense of humour must have been a saving grace. Her books and letters are lit up by it, and it is one of her characteristics that I recall from contact with her as a small child. It was a wry, ironic, at times mocking trait, enabling her, as I now realise, to survive her frustration and suffering. She poked fun at her husband; indirectly, in her books, openly in her letters, and sometimes in her speech. Once, some years after the burning, when I had a bad cold and was relegated by my mother to a nasty little room in the attic next to the hot water tank, Granny, who was visiting us, came up to see me. The tank gurgled and spluttered, rumbled and groaned. 'It's a bit frightening, Granny,' I said. Granny smiled. 'Nonsense,' she replied, 'it sounds exactly like your grandfather eating his porridge!'

Her visits to us were eagerly anticipated, not least because of a wonderful game she invented for us which I now see was very revealing. Ours was a conventional, well-ordered establishment, kept up by a staff that was modest for the privileged by contemporary standards, huge to modern eyes. Brass glittered, windows shone, stable yards were models of tidiness and there was fresh paint everywhere.

Granny's game was called Muckski. This was not long after the Russian Revolution but the association of ideas was lost on us. The fun consisted in everyone having a toy bucket and spade with which we went round the outside premises collecting mud, dirty water, old leaves, pond slime, spilled motor oil and worse; anything really mucky we could find. You then put the whole lot together in a larger bucket, presided over by Granny, and took your turn in mixing it all up with a large stick. The climax to this delightful occupation consisted in stealing a paintbrush from the potting shed and carrying out the solemn ritual of plastering every door and gate within range with the oozy, greyish liquid. By this time our neat tweed coats and shiny wellington boots (Nanny's idea of playwear) were usually covered with the stuff, and we all, including Granny, revelled in the mess we had made. No one could remonstrate, because of Granny. I am sure Muckski was a tease, disguised as a game to amuse the children. A psychologist friend of mine is fascinated by this activity, and convinced that it is revealing on another level, that of the unconscious. He sees Milly as projecting her fury and resentment at her lot in life into this essentially dirty and disruptive, if harmless, ritual.

It is sad that Milly seems not to have been able to surmount her misery, humorous and brave though she certainly was. Her frustration must have been enormous, but she was gifted with such powerful inner resources that one might have expected her to have found a little happiness outside her predicament. If her letters are to be believed, this was not so. Carl Jung maintained that an understanding, however flawed, of the meaning of one's sufferings made them bearable. I doubt if Milly ever came to terms with hers; they may well have been worse than we can imagine. I recall her smile, but have no recollection of having ever heard her laugh. In a letter to Sydney Carroll, undated, but probably written in 1917, she writes: 'So glad to have my Diana out of this home sweet home for I know *she* would not stand seeing violent hands laid on her Mother, would remonstrate, maybe try to defend me, with result they would be turned on her, she possibly resist instead of being as I am a perfectly passive, inert, rather bored body...' Perhaps there is a clue here, a hint of what Milly had become, after years of ill-treatment. Much earlier, in her story 'An April Fool', she has the doctor, Richard Meara, tortured by a miserable marriage, confide to the heroine of the tale: 'One must be alive to feel pain.'[7] If Milly herself speaks through these words, as I believe she does, this infinitely sorrowful observation says it all, for one must also be alive to feel joy. That gloomy word resignation rears its head again. It is a word that has no link with understanding or overcoming; the 'virtue' of resignation lies in the suffering it occasions.

To what extent Milly was the victim of her own nature and upbringing or was crippled emotionally by her association with Jonathan Darby we shall never know, but there are indications in the next chapter that her alienation from him was intensified by her supernatural experiences in the castle.

7 p. 157.

7
The Ghosts

'Perhaps there is no house in the world that holds so many suggestions of the supernatural. Leap has to be seen to be believed.' Those are the words of Sacheverell Sitwell, who visited Leap in the early Thirties and wrote about it in his book of essays, *Dance of the Quick and the Dead.*[1] Some sixty years on, the mere mention of the place still evokes a dramatic response among cognoscenti of the paranormal, as my daughter discovered quite recently. She was dining with some acqaintances interested in unexplained phenomena such as ghosts, and not unnaturally she made some reference to Leap. The effect was electric. One member of the party dropped his fork and exclaimed that Leap Castle was probably the most haunted house in Europe.

The ghosts of Leap indeed attracted worldwide attention for most of the twentieth century. Distinguished Irish writers have been fascinated by them, and countless articles in newspapers and periodicals have enumerated and described them over and over again. Add to this the perennial folkloric exchanges in the neighbourhood on the subject, and it is apparent that we have here a narrative that will not lie down.

I have not encountered any mention of the Leap ghosts before the latter part of the nineteenth century, but apparently there were rumours about them before that. Miss Anna Stoney, a neighbour of the Darbys whose family were prominent Brethren, had evidently heard some of these tales. She relates in her unpublished memoirs that she had discussed the ghosts with John Nelson Darby himself, who thought it quite possible that evil deeds might attract the devil to the scene of the crimes. The writers of *The New Handbook of Ireland,* who painted such a rosy picture of Leap a generation earlier, naively remarked that 'It would be strange if Leap Castle were not haunted…'. They add: 'Stories are told of … most extraordinary and unaccountable apparitions….' None are then described, but both this and other contemporary articles indicate that assumptions about the hauntings had taken root in earlier days. The supposed existence of ghosts at the castle was

1 Faber & Faber (London, 1936), p. 9.

mentioned in the newspaper account of my grandparents' homecoming after their wedding in 1889. However, it was not until the new Mrs Darby wrote about them that they became famous. It was undoubtedly she who set the ball rolling.

My grandmother, as newspaper reporters who met her are at pains to assert, was not an airy-fairy sort of person, prone to fits of the vapours and habitually at the mercy of her fantasies. She was a hunting, shooting and fishing country lady, who happened also to be a novelist. She lived in a castle that everyone thought was haunted, yet in all her time there she herself saw only one ghost. Of the rest, she was merely the chronicler.

Milly had not been married for more than a couple of years when an account of her first sighting was written up by a friend of hers in the 1881 Christmas Number of the *Review of Reviews*, and this was reproduced in an article in the *Midland Tribune* on 13 February 1892. Leap itself is not mentioned by name, nor is Milly. Under the heading 'An Irish Castle and Its Ghosts', this is the earliest specific account of the hauntings that I have come across. It precedes by some sixteen years the publication of Milly's own initial record of the ghosts, and includes a vivid description of the one later known as The Elemental. The lady of the house is reported to have seen this one, and no mention is made of any previous sightings of it. Milly must have sanctioned this thinly veiled disclosure, which, if Jonathan got to hear of the article, probably exacerbated the already existing marital strife about the ghosts of Leap.

According to my mother and aunts, Granny's dramatic accounts of the Leap hauntings infuriated her irascible husband from quite early on. He accused his young wife of deliberately trying to frighten the life out of the household and forbade her to speak of the subject. When anyone mentioned the ghosts of Leap, he would angrily deny their existence. 'The only spirits in this house', he would, according to my mother, declare, 'are in the cellars.' Milly put up with this ridicule for years before she decided to do something about it: she wove the old rumours as well as her own horrific experiences into a story, with, let it be admitted, every appearance of relish. The earlier account pales into insignificance.

Milly's tale was entitled 'Kilman Castle, the House of Horror'. It was published in the *Occult Review* in December 1908. The setting is Kilman Castle in the west of Ireland during a shooting party, in which Milly features as Betty, the hostess, and Jonathan as Maurice, the host. It is told, in Milly's characteristic 'Andrew Merry' style, by a forthright and steady soldier on leave, Captain Gordon, who she claims is based on one of her brothers. Another male guest, called Adair, and an amusingly drawn *jeune fille*, petite, dimpled and given to frothy chat, play minor parts in the narrative. The story reveals a *penchant* for the sensational that might be expected in so frustrated a person who was also a novelist.

In 'Kilman Castle', Captain Gordon, on his journey from the train, hears the old family coachman relate the tale of Finola O'Carroll and Captain Darby, with no names mentioned, followed by an account of the dastardly deeds of the Wild Captain. Then follows a minute description of Leap itself, inside and out, that is so exact as to make the identity of 'Kilman Castle' indisputable. All the guests are now assembled in the castle, and Milly inserts into the scene of this house-party a number of conversations between Betty and the Captain, as well as some shocking experiences undergone by the other visitors, which furnish an account of almost every ghostly manifestation ever heard of at Leap. Since then, each one of these has become part of the whole saga, surfacing, with variations, over and over again, woven into the legends, so that what was in fact collated and described with such gusto by the last Mrs Darby of Leap in the twentieth century has assumed the character of timeless folklore.

I cannot imagine how Milly, however desperate to be heard, had the courage to let the cat out of the bag in that way. Grandfather knew nothing about the existence of 'Kilman Castle' until it appeared in print. He was both shocked and furious, so I was told. For a start, though this was a mere detail, he found the criticism of himself, in the character of Maurice O'Connell, insupportable. Milly sets this scene after dinner at Kilman Castle when Betty has gone up to bed, and Captain Gordon inquires whether there are any ghosts in the old place. Maurice denies it:

> 'If anything makes me really mad, it's the rot people talk about spirits and apparitions in this house.'
>
> 'What says Betty to all these things? Does she listen to such folly?'
>
> My host pulled angrily at his pipe ... before he replied:
>
> 'She got some idiotic maggot in her brain last year, and has turned ever since as nervous as a cat. It's too bad of her; I did think she had some common sense, that was why I married her.'

No husband would have been best pleased at this pen picture of himself; to my grandfather it would have been an intolerable impertinence.

But much worse was to come. Behind this most transparent of disguises, Leap itself was decried – presented as a 'House of Horror'. Milly's lurid story quickly became hot news, which in turn gave rise to the unwelcome attentions of psychic investigators. Jonathan was by now beside himself with rage. Try as he would to keep the lid on this kettle of fish, his beloved home was exposed to public scrutiny of the most outrageous kind. Moreover, his wife was suddenly a celebrity, and what could be more distasteful than that? He never forgave her.

After the above highly entertaining preamble, Milly gets going on the ghost stories, starting off with an incident that in had fact happened to her.

It is the dead of night at Kilman Castle when Captain Gordon is awakened by a terrified little dog. He puts out his hand to calm it, and finds another icy hand in his, followed by a loud bump, as of a falling body, as the hand lets go. Absolute stillness is followed by 'a deep human groan, and some half articulated words, or, to be accurate, prayers'.

Captain Gordon, a stout-hearted military man, lights his candle and searches the room. On bending down to look under the bed, he notices that his hand, resting on the floor, has encountered something damp:

> I held it close to the light, and saw my finger-tips and the ball of my thumb were reddened as if with blood, and turning back the rug I discovered a dark stain, extending perhaps for two feet one way, and three or four the other.

In the morning the stain is still there, but quite dry.

The next day Captain Gordon tells Betty what occurred, and she admits that he is not the first person to have had that experience. She explains that in that room, called the Muckle or Murder Hole room (a direct reference to Leap), a man slew his brother, the priest, at prayer, and the dying victim laid a curse on his killer, that no eldest son should ever inherit the castle and estate.[2] Here Milly has rolled two Leap stories into one, which was naughty of her, as the tales themselves purported to be the gospel truth, albeit in a fictional setting.

So much, for the time being, for the bloodstain. Milly is only just getting into her stride as the chronicler of horrors. We are regaled by a drunken steward rolling barrels down a flight of stairs, a shrieking

2 This detail is an embroidery, lending colour to the fact that so many first-born male Darbys in line of succession (five in a row, at one point) failed to inherit. In any event, the murder of the priest traditionally occurred in the Bloody Chapel, during Mass.

damsel in a scarlet dress rushing through the castle pursued by two lustful brothers,[3] a sly-looking cleric, a groaning nobleman stuck up a chimney (pure pantomime), and several more, which I shall describe later. These colourful spectres, presumably already thought to exist at Leap, and entertainingly recorded here by Milly, frequently crop up in conversation with the neighbours to this day.

I can imagine the excitement that Milly must have felt when her storyteller's artistry decreed that the time was ripe to introduce her own ghost. Considered too revolting to name, for a name affirms identity, this being was always referred to as 'The Thing', or just 'It'. In 'Kilman Castle' Betty describes 'It' to Captain Gordon.

> 'Suddenly, two hands were laid on my shoulders. I turned round sharply and saw... a grey 'Thing' standing a couple of feet from me, with its bent arms raised, as if it were cursing me. I cannot describe in words how utterly awful the 'Thing' was, its very undefinableness rendering the horrible shadow more gruesome. Human in shape, a little shorter than I am, I could just make out the shape of big black holes like eyes and sharp features, but the whole figure — head, face, hands and all — was grey — unclean, bluish grey, something of the colour and appearance of common cotton wool. But oh! so sinister, repulsive, and devilish. My friends who are clever about occult things say it is what they call an "Elemental".'

Later in the story, Captain Gordon himself is confronted by The Thing when it accosts him at his bedroom door. He gives a picture of its appearance through his eyes:

> The Thing was about the size of a sheep, thin gaunt and shadowy in parts. Its face was human, or to be more accurate, inhuman, in its vileness, with large holes of blackness for eyes, loose, slobbery lips and a thick saliva-dripping jaw, sloping back suddenly into its neck. Nose it had none, only spreading cancerous cavities, the whole face being one uniform tint of grey. This too was the colour of the dark coarse hair covering its head, neck and body. Its forearms were thickly coated with the same hair, so were its paws, large, loose and hand shaped; as it sat on its hind legs, one hand or paw was raised ready to scratch the paint. Its lustreless eyes, which seemed half decomposed in black cavities and looked

3 In one version, the lady, an O'Carroll, is fleeing to the arms of her lover and 'leaps' from the battlements. Miss Anna Stoney records this tale in her memoirs.

> incredibly foul, stared into mine, and the horrible smell which before had offended my nostrils, only a hundred times intensified, came up into my face, filling me with a deadly nausea. I noticed that the lower half of the creature was indefinite, and seemed semi-transparent — at least, I could see the framework of the door that led into the gallery through its body.

The touch of macabre humour implicit in the observation about scratching the paint sounds more like Milly than Captain Gordon, and this is the first mention of the vile smell emanating from the spectre, later to become such a feature.

This spine-chilling and marvellously lively Andrew Merry story, of which I have given the merest outline, ends on a note of high drama. Captain Gordon, confronted by The Elemental, falls down in a faint, and Nell, the little dog that had been so put out by the bloodstain, drops dead with terror.

Hard, in this instance, not to sympathise with Jonathan Darby. Who would not hate the implication that phantoms, including a hideous, evil being that could both touch and exude a stench, were at large in a much-loved ancestral home?

There is another record of Milly's supernatural experiences. This consists of twenty-one items: letters, postcards and photographs sent by her to a Mr Sydney Carroll in London, in 1917 and 1918, and again in 1922, after the burning. It includes many of the same stories as those published some ten years before, but with more emphasis on Jonathan's lack of either sympathy or understanding.

Why did Milly need to write another account of the ghosts of Leap? And why did she choose to lodge this with a mere acquaintance who bore the name of her husband's supposed ancestors? We can only guess at her motive. My conjecture is that once the furore caused by 'Kilman Castle' had died down, at least for the time being, Milly feared that her assertions would cease to have any credibility and be forgotten. Perhaps people were already saying that she made the whole thing up: as one journalist put it later, 'Mrs Darby knew how to spin a yarn.' What were to her very important facts had to be put on record again, and lodged with a reliable source for posterity. Sydney Carroll must have agreed to act in this capacity, for the documents are carefully collated and preserved, as Milly wished. This time she wrote in the first person, and enclosed a number of photographs and documents.

This correspondence consists of five letters, from some of which pages are tantalisingly missing, perhaps not by accident. Only one or two are dated, but they were definitely written in 1917 and in 1922. Here my grandmother gives vent to her thoughts on a number of subjects concerning Ireland and the nature of the Irish, but her main concern in the earlier ones is the ghosts of Leap. Clearly, these letters to Mr Carroll allowed her to unburden herself, without, as she explains to him, breaking her written word not to publish. This, promise, it will be recalled, had been extracted from Milly by her husband in 1909. She must have sent the letters without Jonathan's knowledge and presumably she burned Mr Carroll's replies.

The opening letter begins, with characteristic irony: 'You are a man of the world and therefore know a bit about the dangers of allowing the inferior sex to start in talking…' Thereafter, the tales begin. The Muckle Hole story is, in this account, related as follows:

> The incident of Easter early between 2 and 3 a.m…was this. Sleeping the sleep of the just, usually in his case a very sound one, we were both awakened by the noise of a very heavy fall and two or three groans coming from the room next mine, the Muckle or Murder Hole Room. At once I was ordered to get up and see what had caused the noise, cursing at blank blank dogs of the weaker sex, i.e. servants up to some larks or 'one of <u>my</u> pictures, you have cut the cord, probably'.
>
> I lit candle, went into the room, empty furniture just as usual, when taking a few steps to be sure pictures were safely on walls my bare foot – had not waited to look for slippers – stepped on something warm and moist. I looked down to see the dark usually dry stain on the old oak boards wet, and my foot much blood stained. <u>Nothing</u> visible beyond this. Back to my own room saying I could see no fallen picture … wiped my foot and made no remark as to it. 'You'll be trying to say of your blank blank rot of ghosts I suppose, when for sheer devilment you wake me out of my much needed sleep etc. etc.' continued until he slept again, since not a word on the matter, but more than usual desire to find fault…

Unlike the 'Kilman Castle' account, no mention is made here of any legend in connection with the bloodstain, but my grandfather comes over as a hostile bully, bent on humiliating his wife.

Liquefaction, in various forms, crops up from time to time in hearsay and tradition. There is another Irish tale of this kind, to do with the

Great Rebellion of 1798. Elizabeth, Countess of Fingall, relates in her book *Seventy Years Young*[4] that the ground on a part of the hill of Tara where 4,000 rebels were buried, having been slain by yeomanry troops led by Lord Fingall, is held to be forever damp with the blood of the fallen. She goes on to recall that in our own island history the flagstones of an antechamber in Mary Queen of Scots's apartment in Edinburgh Castle are stained to this day with the blood of her murdered chief advisor, David Rizzio. In a religious connection, statues of saints weep, the Virgin's breasts ooze with milk, blood flows from the Saviour's side on crucifixes. This seems to 'happen' as a reminder to humanity that nothing is ever over and done with, whether secular or sacred, while held in the memory, and it falls to some people, often the very devout, to witness these odd occurrences, perhaps in response to some submerged need.

I am not alone in believing that events can occur spontaneously if the need for them is urgent enough. It is what Shelley means when, in his poem, *Prometheus Unbound,* he urges mankind to 'hope till Hope creates, From its own wreck, the thing it contemplates'. My grandmother, resented by her husband, isolated from congenial companionship, forbidden to publish stories and probably longing for attention, seems to me to have become addicted to the idea of spectral goings-on in her home, willing them into being. Moreover, her evocation of them appears often to have rendered their presence evident to other people, including, I suspect, her husband, who denied their existence with such vehemence. This curious transmission of an intense experience could well account for the incidents involving several people at once. The fact that Milly was not a hysterical woman would make her all the more persuasive.

As if to confute the conclusion that the ghosts were all in her mind, my grandmother tells Sydney Carroll in one of the 1917 letters:

> All my children 'saw' what we did not, constantly until they were 4 or 5, but ... none of them exhibited any sign of fear, speaking with interest and curiosity of what they saw.... They usually spoke enquiring as to who were the lovely lady in red, the funny old man in black with such a shiny head, the little man in green clothes with such beautiful shining things on his shoes, all alike, and sometimes two together saw these.

4 First published by Collins of London, 1937. Paperback edition, The Lilliput Press, 1991. p. 109.

I am not convinced by this. One of these harmless spectres, the little man in green, was mentioned as early as 1892, in the story from that Christmas Number of the *Review of Reviews* while Milly was still childless. Moreover, they had all been described almost word for word in 'Kilman Castle', but without reference to the children, which suggests that Milly had seen or at least described them first. However, in that account Betty remarks to Captain Gordon:

> 'There is something that very young children see and no one else. Fortunately, as the children grow out of babyhood they seem to lose the power of seeing this thing. My babies saw it when they were too young to talk, and were sent precious nearly into convulsions.'

This is in contradiction to Milly's subsequent remark in a letter to Sydney Carroll that 'none of them exhibited any signs of fear'. It looks as if she put in the bit about terrified babies in 'Kilman Castle'to add a *frisson* to the tale, which leads one to suspect that she was not averse to a little deliberate embroidery.

Milly's children, accustomed to the idea of ghosts, all told their own offspring that from time to time a monk-like figure in a black habit and cowl would wander through their schoolroom, which was in the Priest's House. This unthreatening apparition is an obvious one for them to encounter in a part of the castle bearing this evocative name: they had no adult hang-ups to project, only a mild curiosity, as they sat at their lessons in broad daylight. I have no doubt that he was there, for them, probably at the suggestion of their mother.

Monks seem particularly prone to ghostly manifestation in folklore, while in fiction Anton Chekhov, writing in the latter part of the nineteenth century, has a wonderful short story, entitled 'The Black Monk'. The hero, Kovrin, enters into conversation with the monk. 'I'm an apparition...' the monk declares, after describing himself as a product of Kovrin's 'overheated imagination'.

> 'That means you don't exist?' Kovrin asked.
>
> 'Think what you like,' the monk said with a weak smile, 'I exist in your imagination, and your imagination is part of nature, so I exist in nature too.'

Milly would be loth to accept Chekhov's view: she was convinced that the ghosts had a life of their own.

As well as 'the lovely lady in red', said to have been seen by the Darby children, and the poor girl in scarlet being chased by the lecherous brothers, another red ghost is on record, too dramatic to ignore. This one is described in a letter published in the *Occult Review*, (January 1909) following the publication of 'Kilman Castle', alleged to have been addressed to my grandmother by one of her house guests and forwarded by her to the periodical. The writer makes a point of saying that it appeared at 12.45 a.m. on 1 November. November was the month when Milly herself always went away from home, on account of the proliferation of malignant apparitions:

> I was wide awake with an extraordinary cold feeling at my heart that rapidly increased in intensity. Almost immediately I felt, as much as saw, that there was a tall figure in the middle of the room....
>
> 'What is it?' I asked.
>
> There was no answer, but I could now see, dimly at first and then with increasing distinctness, that the tall figure was clothed from head to foot in red, and with its right hand raised menacingly in the air.... To my utter astonishment, I could see that the light which illuminated the figure was from within.... I was convinced that what I saw was supernatural... I could see distinctly that the form was that of a very tall woman, holding some form of weapon, knife or dagger, in her hand.

Whoever laid claim to that particular encounter had a prose style remarkably like that of the chatelaine of Leap, almost as if the letter had been dictated.

I imagine that a red ghost, rather like a red devil, would be particularly alarming to encounter: the colour red is associated with danger. It is also thought to arouse rage, as in bullfighting. And let us not forget about the ghostly blood, and its grim association with violence. I have no doubt that psychologists would see a relationship between Milly's varying states of mind and the different ghosts that she either described or encountered, just as they tell us that all our dreams are about ourselves.

As for alfresco ghosts, in Betty's words 'they swarm'. This is a telling verb in the context, suggesting an unearthly hum emanating from jostling entities. It is odd that no mention is made here of the inconsolable shade of the Wild Captain, wringing its skeletal hands as it searched the castle grounds for the hidden treasure.

The Elemental is widely regarded as the most interesting of the entities at Leap. It is also the most famous, still referred to in hushed tones by several of the people living near Leap to whom I spoke. I have already recorded Milly's two descriptions of The Thing in 'Kilman Castle', but yet another encounter with it is described in one of Milly's letters to Sydney Carroll. Again, several people are with her who are all said to have seen it, and on this occasion my grandfather is reported to have been convulsed with anger and (says Milly) fear, accusing her of setting the spectacle up to frighten everyone. This time she herself experienced only the foul stink, but she reports that everyone who saw and smelt the apparition was violently sick. My mother told me that after this Milly was ill with shock for a fortnight.

Instances of spirit entities that smell have been recorded elsewhere. In his fascinating book *Holy Ghostbuster*,[5] the Revd J. Aelwyn Roberts has a story of one such, while Rosamond Lehmann, writing about the death of her daughter Sally in *The Swan in the Evening*,[6] describes most eloquently the beautiful scent that filled the room whenever she felt Sally's presence. It is not surprising that if the mind can conjure up life-like entities it can also imagine a vile smell or a heady fragrance so powerfully that it evokes a physical response.

'The Thing' seems to be a personification of fear and self-disgust. Half animal, half human, dirty, nebulous, reeking, it is the epitome of shame, as perceived in the consciousness of a sensitive person brought up in a Victorian Evangelical family. It might also indicate repressed or even unconscious desire: that it actually touched Milly may not be without significance. It appears that Milly projected this image so powerfully that the experience was transmitted to others, since no one seems to have encountered the creature unless she was nearby, if not actually on the spot. Like Captain Gordon in the story, Milly's son Horatio is reported to have shot at it several times with a pistol, to no avail. It is said that he fainted, which seems very unlikely for a soldier in the Irish Guards, and a typical example of the Darby tendency to over-egg the pudding. Several people have asserted that The Elemental is the ghost of an O'Carroll who died of leprosy in the castle, having been locked up in isolation for many years. This too sounds like an accretion, albeit an ingenious one, to lend authenticity to the supposed sightings and smell.

5 Robert Hale Ltd, 1990, ch. 9, p. 76.
6 Collins, 1967.

Before leaving the subject of The Elemental, mention must be made of William Butler Yeats's[7] and of Oliver St John Gogarty's[8] writings about it – an indication of the widespread fascination in which this odd entity was held, years after my grandmother's disclosures, by the intelligentsia as well as others. Each of these writers saw, in this haunting, deep metaphorical undertones, and brought their respective literary skills to bear upon the tale. Neither had, so far as we know, any direct contact with my grandmother, and her letter to Sydney Carroll quoted on page 107, seems to bear this out. Rather, the two relied heavily on anecdotal evidence, which proliferated as time went on. The paranormal is so vague an area that liberties can all too easily be taken with such 'data' as exists, the stories getting altered a little here and there to fit theories as to their meaning. Neither Yeats nor Gogarty was above taking such liberties.

A fascinating essay by Grover Smith, an American academic, throws light on the respective contributions of these writers to the debate on a subject that is still, in occult circles, alive and well. Entitled 'Yeats, Gogarty and The Leap Castle Ghost', this essay forms part of a collection published by the Iona College Press, New York, entitled *Modern Irish Literature*.[9] Mr Smith quotes from both men's contributions, illustrating the extent to which their interpretations as well as their material about The Elemental differed, according to the requirements of the literary form they each employed. I shall not reiterate here what Mr Smith has so perceptively and elegantly laid out in his essay, but will draw on some of his observations.

Gogarty introduced a note of magic into his offering (entitled 'The Most Haunted House of Them All')[10] when he repeated a version told to him by someone in Roscrea in which The Thing is averred to be a woman who was turned into a ram. Inevitably, a sexual connotation then creeps into the story. What had been reported by Milly as The Thing putting its paws on her shoulders resurfaces as an attempt by the creature to violate a visitor as he ascends what Gogarty dramatically describes as 'the great stair', before making away 'with a scamper of hoofs'. His account is a progression from Milly's and hovers precariously on the boundary between the repulsive and the comic. Why has

7 1865–1939.
8 1878–1957.
9 Published in 1972 and edited by R. J. Porter and J. D. Brophy with the sub-title 'Essays in Honor of William York Tindall, pp. 129–41.
10 From his book *A Week in the Middle of the Week, and Other Essays on the Bias* (New York, 1958), pp. 202–9.

the victim become a man? Possibly, in the male-oriented climate of the era, to sound more convincing, if not actually more titillating? Be that as it may, as often happens when a myth evolves, this version may just possibly have some relevance to Milly's actual experience, undisclosed in her own description of The Thing. She would not have been the first unsuspecting woman to feel debased by the nature of her husband's advances, but she did live at a time when such a subject was unmentionable and might therefore fulminate in the mind, expressing itself obliquely. The Elemental may have represented not only shame, guilt and hidden desire, as I have already suggested, but a specific kind of humiliation as well.

Yeats did not write of The Elemental until 1937. He is more ambitious and profound in his treatment of the story. He was steeped in the world of myth and magic, of ghosts and fairies, that has coloured the consciousness of the Irish people for all time, but he was also involved in the debate about the after-life that was currently in vogue at that time, which drew upon spiritualism and mysticism. He uses what he calls 'the Leap Ghost' to illustrate an abstruse point about the soul's progress towards reincarnation, in his work *A Vision,*[11] in which he describes what he sees as the six states from death to rebirth, a subject outside the scope of this book. He accepts that the spectre was half human, half animal, but omits the magical, transmogrifying element introduced by Gogarty, treating The Elemental's appearance and vile breath as allegorical.[12]

On the whole, Yeats's general comments about folk-beliefs in Ireland are more relevant to our subject. In his Introduction to *Irish Fairy Folk Tales,* he makes the following observation: 'Each county has usually some family or personage supposed to have been favoured or plagued, especially by phantoms...'[13] He also asserts, in his chapter on ghosts, that 'the souls of the dead sometimes take the shape of animals',[14] which is interesting in view of the sheeplike aspect of The Elemental.

One of the Leap apparitions that Milly does not record is a harsh-faced warder, lurking near the Bloody Chapel. He was often mentioned in my hearing, and may be a latecomer to the spectral gathering. It is intriguing that as a small child, my cousin Johnnie recalled the sudden appearance of a stern figure at the door of the long-disused chapel,

11 1937.

12 Yeats associates the smell with that of the charnel house, or repository for the dead, and this detail surfaces in many later versions of the tale.

13 The full title is *Fairy and Folk Tales of the Irish Peasantry*, edited and selected by W. B. Yeats (Walter Scott Ltd, London, n.d.), p. xi.

14 Ibid., p. 129.

where the little boy had gone to play with his bow and arrow. The strangely-dressed man told him he had no business to be there, and Johnnie, suddenly very cold and frightened, left the place hurriedly. The episode made an impression on my cousin deep enough to be vivid, still, in his eighties. Perhaps that lonely boy had fallen under the spell of the place and become caught up in some fantasy of his own, conceivably based on below-stairs gossip, overheard and remembered.

What of animal hauntings? They can show symptoms of being aware of ghosts. Milly's horses would freeze with terror at unexpected moments and her dogs and all others in the vicinity would bark wildly, their hackles bristling, promptly at 11.30 each evening. Had Milly or some predecessor evoked or created whatever disturbed them, or were they susceptible to her apprehensions? And why was it that hounds would never run across the demesne land of the castle? At least, that is what the locals say. Foxes, it seems, were less choosy, unless, being creatures of the dark themselves, they were considered not to be at odds with the spirits. There are more recent reports of dogs suddenly going berserk. Seán Ryan's little terrier does so sometimes when he is at work in the castle. The name Aghancon means, in Irish, 'the field of the hound' and it is possible that this is relevant. Aghancon is, after all, very close to Leap. Could there be canine ghosts at large? It seems more likely that some atmospheric condition may suddenly disturb dogs in the same way that it can disturb human beings, but I do not rule out the possibility that past events could have something to do with this, and with all animal eccentricities of behaviour in this context, since we can safely assume that animals have no imagination.

Leap Castle's air of mystery, sadness and latent power is indisputable. It has an immense exterior presence, while inside the house, the oubliette, the bones in the dungeons and the skeletons walled in for hundreds of years were physical evidence of past violence of which more recent inhabitants must always have been vaguely aware. The double walls and blocked-up rooms would have had an unsettling effect on the imaginative, while the presence of many large mirrors would have given rise to odd effects in some conditions, particularly in the flickering light of candles or the hissing vibrations of gaslight. Moreover, it must always have had dark, sinister and probably damp areas, even when it was full of furniture and people. The gallery, too, is significant. Hanging in mid-air, it seems to feature in most appearances of The Elemental, emphasising by its placement between floor and vaulted ceiling the hybrid nature of the apparition. It was here, too, that my great-grandmother saw her son on the night that he was fatally wounded in France, an episode that I shall describe more fully later in this chapter.

Yeats, again in his book *Irish Fairy Folk Tales*, remarks that: 'Ghosts, or as they are called in Ireland *Thershi* or *Tash*, live in a state intermediary between this life and the next. They are held there by some earthly longing or affection, or some duty unfulfilled, or anger against the living... Those who die suddenly, more commonly than others, are believed to become haunting ghosts.'[15] They would feel at home in a gallery. My mother had a strange story that involved the gallery at Leap. Others besides myself recall her telling it.

In the early days of the Great War, Diana was at home, awaiting instructions to join a Red Cross unit as a trainee nurse. There were many troops stationed in the area, and some of the officers from the nearby garrison, whom the Darbys had befriended, used regularly to bicycle out to Leap for tennis parties. On one of these occasions they were invited to stay for dinner, after which one of the young men, known to be a good musician, was prevailed upon to play for the rest of the party on the grand piano in the drawing room. He told Granny that it had been a rare pleasure to be able to play a piano like that when he was taken up with his military duties. She invited him to come again, and to use it whenever he liked.The party had continued until rather late, and it was pitch dark when the guests set off on bicycles for their barracks.

Some hours later, when she was in bed in the Priest's House, my mother woke to hear distant strains of piano music coming from below. Assuming sleepily that the soldier must have returned, she crept into the gallery to listen to the same lovely pieces he had played earlier. She wondered vaguely why no one else had been woken, but they had dined well after strenuous tennis, and doubtless everyone was 'out for the count'. Eventually the music ceased and Diana, not wanting to be seen in her night clothes, went back to bed. In the morning the news came that the men had been ambushed and shot dead in one of the nearby lanes, as they pedalled back to their unit.

Was this event Diana's response to a premonition? We shall never know. It bears no relation to any of the ghost stories, and is mysterious rather than sinister. It is nevertheless a memorable tale, and it may well have been the ambience of Leap that allowed the incident to present itself to the girl who was to be my mother. I also wonder whether that

15 *Fairy and Folk Tales of the Irish Peasantry*, p. 523.

young man was perhaps thinking of my beautiful mother when sudden death eclipsed him, causing some telepathic vibration that transmitted itself to Diana. Youth and death are uneasy bedfellows and there are many tales of young people seeming to hover in a kind of limbo before succumbing to the extinction of their life force. One I remember was of a woman who woke up to find several fireman sitting on her bed. She talked to them for a while before they disappeared, and read in the paper the next day of a huge local fire that had claimed the lives of some of the firefighters.

There are an increasing number of people who ask for help in getting rid of their ghosts. Exorcism is no longer the exclusive preserve of the priesthood, although many modern 'ghostbusters' work under the aegis of a man or woman of God. Lay people can learn to do this work. The accepted procedure is to address the alleged entity as an unquiet spirit and invite it to depart towards a beckoning light, where it will rest in God's peace. This rarely fails to rid the premises of the supposed unwelcome presence, if carried out with humility and conviction, provided the exorcist has the cooperation of the people who live there. Should they not really want to be rid of their haunter, their thoughts will betray them, the entity will 'return', and the ghostbuster will be called incompetent. It is revealing that Milly pronounced ineffective the exorcism carried out at her husband's behest by a Catholic priest (he did not think the Protestant parson up to the job).[16] Since he professed to disbelieve in the ghosts, it is probable that Jonathan admitted the priest in the hope that it would end all the fuss. It did not. Only my grandmother could do that.

What of the other ghosts of Leap? After Milly had caused such a stir with the publication of 'Kilman Castle', more tales almost inevitably emerged from amongst the neighbouring people, with a proliferation of ghoulish details. Often these were 'improvements' on the originals. One such was concerned with The Elemental, providing it with an ignominious end. The local priest was credited in this account with catching The Thing, putting it in a bottle, and burying it in a deep, squelchy hole near the castle grounds.[17] But The Elemental got its own back. When the priest returned home, he was found to have become an old man, his face grey and sunken and his hair quite white. Grandfather's assertion that the only spirits on the place were in bottles has acquired a *double entendre* from this creepy-hilarious addendum. The

16 Reported in a letter from Milly to Sidney Carroll.
17 Michael, in '*The Dead Coach*' recollections.

bloodstain story, too, is given a makeover. A small, yellowing, newspaper cutting, completely unidentifiable, that has come my way speaks of '... a remarkable room, which none of the servants will enter after nightfall. It was the State Bedroom of one of the princesses of Ely, who was murdered six centuries ago by her lord, and the solid oak floor retains the blood stains of the royal victim.'

Before Leap was burned down, young girls employed as maids did indeed, as legend asserts, refuse to go into some of the rooms at nightfall. They gave in their notice frequently, offering some trumped-up excuse for their departure, and to this day no one likes to pass by the entrance on any night in November. This was the month when, it will be recalled, the ghosts were believed to be so active that Milly always went away from home. Lights were said to shine from the windows of the blocked-up rooms, from which, on occasion, shrieks would pierce the air. My grandfather said that phosphorescence in the stone was responsible for the shining and that owls did the shrieking.

Recorded by Milly in 'Kilman Castle' was a ghost that threw you out of bed. In another version, this entity lay heavily down beside you, leaving a visible impress on the bedclothes. One of these accounts is said to have been vouchsafed by a visiting bishop, and a nurse in charge of a sick person at Leap reputedly gave in her notice because this ghost made so much work for her. My Aunt Cis refers to it in a letter to Mr George Cunningham, remarking: 'I once had all the bedclothes removed to a heap in the middle of the room ... other people had much the same experience and were thrown out of bed.' Dream specialists aver that this is a common form of nightmare, utterly real at the time, which may happen during one of the periods of 'rapid eye movement' sleep that occur several times in a normal night, when the sleeper is in an altered state of consciousness as opposed to the inert condition of deep sleep. When is a ghost not a ghost? In this letter my aunt goes on to mention the 'hair-raising tales' her mother would tell, and adds that as children they just accepted them, and that 'like most children, we adored our old home'.

Less sanguine, it seems, were the young Parsonses of Birr Castle. The present Earl of Rosse told me that his father vividly recalled several children's tea parties at Leap. Apparently, just as they were all beginning to have fun round the big dining table, my grandmother would stiffen and motion to everyone to be quiet. 'Don't stir,' she would admonish them. 'Don't utter a sound! The Thing is here!' The wretched little visitors, as well as the children of the house, who a moment before had been chatting over their sandwiches, froze obediently and in trepidation. After what seemed an age, my grandmother would give a deep sigh, evidently of relief. 'All right, you can talk again now. It's gone,' she would announce, but a thorough damper had been put on the fun and the children could hardly wait to be allowed to leave the tea table and rampage together round the garden.

Just what was Milly up to? Was she having a little game at the expense of the children? That seems more than likely, in view of what we already know about her, and does introduce another note of caution on the validity of many of her allegations.

In about 1916 my grandmother's terrifying (and, one begins to suspect, thrilling) encounters, which had distressed her for so long, came to an end at last. One of her letters to Sydney Carroll, dated February 1917, in which some of the ghosts of Leap are described, concludes with the assertion that, on the advice of Miss Bates, a medium, Milly had taken to praying for the souls of the unquiet spirits and had finally found herself unafraid of them. She explains to Sydney that her husband's dead brother, a sailor,[18] had sent her instructions to this effect via Miss Bates, and adds that a similar exhortation had come to her from her own brother[19] via another mediumistic friend, a Mr Stead. Milly continues her letter as follows: 'Need I add that I have obeyed ever since and all terror of the poor things has completely vanished...'

There is something suspiciously facile about this assertion. Had it never previously occurred to my grandmother, with her strict religious upbringing, that prayer might help? It is more probable that, like those who pronounce a 'ghostbuster' unsuccessful in dismissing resident entities from their homes, she was not at that time ready to let go of her ectoplasmic fellow-inhabitants of the castle. She had, after all, herself denied the efficacy of priestly intervention in the past. Could it be that, at long last, she had had her fill of ghosts and was therefore ready to renounce them? If so, the change of attitude would have taken place at an unconscious level. She would have believed implicitly that it was mediumistic intelligence that guided her.

In another letter to Sydney, undated, my grandmother speaks further of her interest in mediums and in other occult means of communication with the dead, including the then very fashionable 'planchette'. This

18 Burke does not record that any of Jonathan's brothers or half brothers were sailors.

19 Milly had by this time lost two brothers, Robert, a surgeon, and George, a barrister. She told Sydney that the one in question was the Captain Gordon of her story, but does not say which brother this was.

Irish warriors, Albrecht Dürer, 1521

LEFT Irish horseman, engraving RIGHT Irish soldier, by Caspar Rutz, 1588

LEFT Admiral George Darby (1722–90), engraved by H. R. Cook RIGHT R. Earlom engraving (1801) from Sir W. Beechey's portrait of Captain Henry d'Esterre Darby

Lithograph of 'The Leap: The Seat of Admiral Sir Henry Darby K.C.B.'

Mildred Henrietta Gordon Darby, *née* Dill (author's grandmother), in court dress

Milly's parents' Golden Wedding, 1907. Diana, Cecily and Patricia on left, Horatio seated right.

Author's mother with admirers at Leap during First World War

Author's mother's shoes (see p. 60)

The Castle, 1919

Author's parents' wedding day at Leap, 1919: l to r Horatio, Milly, Patricia, Diana (the bride), Edward Mark Philips (bridegroom), Ronald Bannerman (best man), Jonathan, Cecily

Leap after the burning

The author's grandfather, c. 1933

Peter Bartlett

Seán, Anne and Ciara

consists of a vertical pencil and a sheet of paper on a board with casters which, when one or more people place their fingertips on it, is said to produce messages by automatic writing on its surface. The letter does not mention any particular information allegedly vouchsafed to Milly through these channels; her interest seems rather to meet a need to share her experiences in this field with a trusted confidant. Living, as she seems to have done, in increasing isolation from her husband, and having come to terms with the hauntings that had so mesmerised and distressed her in earlier times, it is not surprising that she latched onto another apparent manifestation of the occult. This would have added an exciting and perhaps comforting dimension to her sad, frustrated life at Leap, and provided a new outlet for her energies. It may also have been a way of cocking a snook at her husband.

It was said by several members of the family that, after the burning, the young Alfred Hitchcock, already a celebrated film director,[20] visited the ruins of Leap at my grandmother's invitation, with a view to collaborating with her over the making of a horror film on the premises. It would be fascinating to know what passed between Milly and Alfred Hitchcock, if they did in fact meet. Of his relationship with his audiences, Hitchcock said, 'They like to put their toe in the cold water of fear.' He also said, 'Drama is life with the dull bits left out.' My grandmother would have heartily agreed with both these observations. In all probability Jonathan put a stop to any possible developments, fearing, perhaps, for his own reputation. In any event, nothing came of that venture.

Yeats, in *Irish Fairy Folk Tales* observes that 'fire is the greatest of enemies to every sort of apparition', but the expectation of ghostly encounters at Leap seems to have persisted after the burning. Johnnie Minchin writes:

> I vaguely remember, in about the mid thirties, my grandfather had an altercation with a man called Brown[21] over something or other relating to the queer happenings that had gone on in the castle. He said to this chap that if he stayed in the castle by himself for twelve hours any night of his own choosing, J.C.D. would give him £1000. Thinking this would be too good to miss, Brown is reputed to have spent an hour or so in the house before he hurriedly left, why, he refused to divulge.

20 1899–1980.
21 Brown is a pseudonym.

This story particularly interests me because it took place after Milly's death in 1932, and suggests that, once she had gone, Jonathan was prepared to acknowledge that there might be supernatural goings-on at Leap, and in this case to exploit them to gratify his schoolboyish sense of humour. Moreover, it ties in with another tale, told to me recently by Richard White-Spunner of Milltown Park, Shinrone, a neighbouring house to Leap where my grandfather spent much of his time as a widower. Richard, in his youth, hero-worshipped Jonathan, who befriended him when the boy came to Milltown in his summer holidays and taught him a lot about fishing, shooting and other country pursuits. Richard vividly recalls a picnic one hot summer evening, organised by my grandfather, on the roof of the ruined castle, with the light-hearted idea that at midnight some ghost might appear. They had an excellent feast, as well as a good deal of alcohol, and as twelve o'clock approached the party fell quiet. The next part of this adventure engraved itself on Richard's mind. Upon the hour, two white owls flew up from the dungeons, circled round the picnickers, and dropped like stones back down again. If this was coincidence, it nevertheless remains a moment of intense solemnity. Richard told me that those night birds, age-old symbols of wisdom in the Graeco-Roman mythology with which educated people of that era would have been familiar, made a visible impression on Jonathan – winged messengers seeming to assert that the bad old days were over.

In Celtic mythology, the owl dwells in or beneath the earth, and is known as 'the night hag' or 'the corpse bird'.[22] There is no telling in which guise, if any, those white birds may have appeared. On the principle that people interpret signs in accordance with their culture, I think we can assume that any sinister implication was lost on those public-school-educated revellers, and hope that, full of wine and wisdom, they made it safely off the roof and down the crumbling spiral staircase to terra firma. Not really a ghost story, this tale nevertheless deserves mention as the last curious event known to have occurred at Leap in the lifetime of any of the Darbys who lived there.

Finally, there is a little anecdote, told to me by Seán Ryan, about two Cherokee Indian ladies who recently visited Leap. On entering the hall they flung themselves down on their faces, so strong were the vibrations that seem to have assailed them. They 'picked up' the presences of a small girl in Elizabethan dress, and two female attendants. Later they

22 J. C. Cooper (ed.), *Encyclopaedia of Traditional Symbols*, 1978.

went to a spot in the grounds where they said one of them was buried. These two visitors, from a culture renowned for psychic sensitivity, deserve to be heard with respect. Ciara, Seán and Ann's daughter, has remarked from time to time on the presence in the castle of a child, whom she has called Charlotte, and I recall my own experience when a child at Leap and wonder whether children, with their light baggage, can become aware of a kind of *alter ego* in atmospheric places like Leap. Charlotte would fill the bill nicely. Perhaps it was the child in each of the two Cherokee ladies that attracted her. Is she a thought form? Can one ever know for sure about ghosts?

I have thought long and deeply about this subject, and shall now venture to offer a few observations of my own about the paranormal, including the Leap ghosts.

No one would be foolhardy enough to claim to know what ghosts are. It is, however, possible to hazard a few observations about them in the light of what we are told today about the nature of both mind and matter. It is known that matter is atomic and vibratory. Solidity is therefore an illusion; a difficult idea to grasp if, as is happening here at this moment, an electrician is trying to drill a hole through a two-foot brick wall. The wall is solid and at the same time not solid. The concept 'reality' has to stretch to accommodate this state of affairs. How does this throw light on hauntings?

When one thinks of a ghost, a picture emerges of a being that is three-dimensional yet ethereal, neither quite opaque nor quite transparent. It is, surely, a creature made up of vibrations, like the brick wall, but lacking the concrete quality that is giving my electrician such a hard time. The ghost is abstract, simultaneously there and not there, just as the wall is solid and not solid. Moreover, since a spectre and a wall may both be said to be vibrational, the gap between abstract and concrete, between mind and matter, is considerably narrower than was hitherto generally realised. Mystics have always known this: St Teresa of Avila, whose spiritual raptures were apt to make her levitate, was said to be so embarrassed by this tiresome tendency that when she was worshipping in church she would clutch the floor-covering to avoid making a spectacle of herself. Indian holy men, or yogis, on the other hand, have such control over their physical being that they often levitate while in deep meditation, but take this mastery of the mind over matter quite for granted. What is normal to them is what we would call paranormal.

Amongst ordinary people, not necessarily very spiritual, there are those known as 'sensitives', who are open to the possibility of paranormal happenings, including encounters with ghosts. These individuals are separate from those who are immune to such happenings and regard them as delusions. Most of us, if we are honest, have a foot in both camps. My great-grandmother, Molly Dill, was a 'sensitive'. Milly Darby, in a letter to my other grandmother, Emily Philips, at the time of my parents' engagement, writes: 'My mother has what is known in Ireland as "the Second Sight", and sees much happiness ahead for them.' I have already mentioned earlier in this chapter that Molly was a visitor at Leap when she 'saw' her son Richard standing in the gallery. This was in October 1918. She knew at once that something had happened to him, and in due course a telegram arrived at Leap from the War Office, announcing that he had been severely wounded in the trenches and had died shortly afterwards. My mother vouched for the truth of that story. Could telepathy have been at work here? Soldiers dying in battle often call for their mothers. I believe that Molly, prompted perhaps by intuition, 'heard' her son and then 'saw' him. He was there and not there.

It is important to remember that so-called paranormal incidents cannot occur without the cooperation, conscious or unconscious, of the subject. When people with whom one has been familiar die, their presence in the mind will gradually fade, but they may re-emerge in the consciousness from time to time, just as if they were still alive on earth. One has thought them back, revived in the memory, present in the imagination. Many a husband or wife, not the least bit 'sensitive', will assure you of their frequent awareness of their dead partner, and from time to time we hear of a progression from this situation, in which some actual exchange takes place between the two. One intelligent friend of mine, with arthritic hands, swears that her late husband returned to open a tin of sardines for her while she wept in frustration in the next room. I dare not disbelieve her. Who can say for certain what actually happened? I would like to think that some sort of vibrational alignment took place that performed the office of a tin opener, at the behest of the departed spouse.

As Milly Darby knew, many terrible events are believed to have occurred at Leap Castle. Whether they did or not, and some certainly did, is, in this context, irrelevant; thought created, or recreated them, not just as vivid pictorial memories but, in this case, as real presences. Thought brought the perpetrators and the victims, actual or fictional, inside the walls, where there was one who, although she may not have known it, waited for them, her pen at hand.

Milly, as I have said, had only two ghostly encounters herself, one with the blood-stain and the other, several times, with The Elemental. We know that, as a result, her life and that of those around her was profoundly affected; but why did she become so obsessed with what happened? Why did she give two separate written accounts of the ghosts, not to mention the early one recorded by her friend in the *Review of Reviews,* giving rise to the countless newspaper articles? All pointed the finger at Leap, House of Horror, hotbed of unquiet spirits, sinister stronghold of the paranormal. What was in it for Milly?

From all accounts, my grandmother, like the prophet Cassandra, was a woman to whom no one at home listened. Although outwardly a conventional country lady, she was different from her neighbours; a writer with worlds revolving inside her mind. Nobody, it seems, came halfway to meet the person seething within that neat Edwardian exterior. Milly was a creative woman shut inside herself, whose friends and relations mostly lived in England. Scorned and abused by her husband, she was never afraid of him. She stuck to her guns about her hauntings, believing in them implicitly and, in defiance of Jonathan, making as much of a drama as possible out of the situation. No roaring, abusive husband would ever make her recant. To me, it is entirely understandable that my grandmother, a 'sensitive', felt the sticky wetness of that blood, knew the touch of The Thing, saw its eye-sockets and smelt its stinking breath. Leap is an extraordinarily powerful house, and, as I discovered outside the chapel door all those years ago, things can happen to you if you deliberately put yourself in its thrall. I was not trying to prove anything, so I kept my ghost quiet. Milly, on the other hand, was fighting all her married life for the survival of her identity, and insisting upon the validity of the ghosts was a vital part of her struggle. Jonathan could stop his wife publishing, but he had no power over the workings of her mind. In that Christmas article of 1891, the writer had referred to my grandmother as 'a young English lady of considerable force of character and originality'. She hung onto those qualities for the whole of her life, aided and abetted, albeit involuntarily, by the Leap ghosts.

In this chapter I had hoped to come off the fence as either a believer or a disbeliever in the ghosts of Leap. As it is, I remain perched on top of it. Nothing that I have read, heard or known convinces me absolutely that the castle ghosts appeared, or indeed could appear, of their own accord. If they did not, it seems reasonable to assume that they were, in the words of Chekhov's Black Monk, the product of 'an overheated imagination' that was powerful enough to attract others into its orbit. Nor do I accept that many of those ghosts, proliferating over the years, ever existed except in ghost stories. And yet, and yet… There are people who have made a lifelong study of the subject who would certainly disagree with me. At moments, I disagree with myself: it seems such a colossal impertinence to suggest that my grandmother, whom I loved, may have been the victim of delusion. Once again in this tale, I suspend my disbelief.

8
The Burning

Leap Castle was burned down on 30 and 31 July 1922, during the short-lived but violent Irish Civil War. This had simmered for some time before coming to a head on 28 June 1922, when Free State forces shelled the Four Courts in Dublin, a seat of government which had been taken over by the 'Irregulars', who opposed the recently signed Peace Treaty, with its compulsory oath of allegiance to England. The country was fired by a fresh hatred of English domination, and the new Free State government, supported in large measure by the Anglo-Irish, was discredited.

The generally accepted version of what led to Leap's destruction was that the action formed part of the uprising of Irish nationalists, one of whose aims was to get rid of the landlords and all that they stood for. Ireland had to be returned to the Irish. It has, over the years, been said by various members of the family without any substantiation that the attack was instigated by agitators from Sligo, by Republicans, by the flying column of one or other IRA, even by a posse of drunken Australian soldiers, but more than one Leap tenant has ruefully admitted recently to having taken part in the burning. It is now known that there were more than a few who lived on the Leap estate who both planned and carried out the deed, albeit on a tide of nationalism whipped up by the local IRA (at that time the militant wing of the anti-Treaty contingent), and in a climate of fear for their own future. A recent account confirms this, as will be seen, but it is entirely understandable that the Darbys should have shied away from the possibility that their own neighbours, many of them employees, could have done so terrible a thing to them. Never averse to a little wishful thinking, they latched onto any other possible culprits.

After the fire the applicant for compensation, my grandfather, is reported by his counsel to have 'suffered at the hands of tyranny', which seems on the face of it to be an ironic description of the experience of Jonathan Darby of Leap. The epithet 'tyrannical' was often ascribed to Jonathan himself, and was not the burning of Leap by local people partly an instance of tit for tat? To be sure, it was generally believed that if the castle were destroyed the Darbys would leave and the people would get the land, but the burning, the looting and the wanton destruction of everything else leads me to consider the perpetrators of the outrage – those underlings who do not belong directly to the history of Leap but who cannot be excluded from its life. They formed the substructure that supported it and were themselves dependent upon it for their livelihood.

That Jonathan's grandfather, William Henry Darby, was a model landlord is undisputed, but he left a number of unpaid repair bills and other debts. This was an added burden on his young successor, who was under threat from the start, with campaigns to get rid of his kind increasing in strength as part of Ireland's drive towards independence. It did not matter whether a person was a good or a bad landlord; as a species, they were already doomed to extinction. In Jonathan's case, the odds were perhaps stacked more heavily against him than they might have been had he been a more overtly lovable character. There is no evidence that he was not, by and large, fair to his tenants; indeed he could not have held responsible positions in the county had he been unjust. But tales of his quick temper, impatience and intolerence are legion in hearsay. There is one case recorded in the *Midland Tribune* (15 September 1900) where the law upheld the eviction from the Leap estate of an eighty-year-old widow, '...whose family preceded her in possession of the little place for the past 200 years, paid her yearly rent, £2, with the greatest regularity.... Mrs Tynan is now cast on the road with her son and daughter. It would be well if Mr. Darby could see his way to reconsider his action in this most deserving and pitiable case.' Strong words from a local newspaper. Johnnie Minchin recalled his grandfather pointing out where he had man-traps concealed around the estate. These consisted of deep, camouflaged pits into which intruders would fall, to be hauled out later by a keeper who doubtless inflicted summary corporal punishment. Such devices, even if in widespread use among landlords, were hardly calculated to promote good relations with the locals. To my grandfather, however, an uprising on the part of his tenants and other villagers was unthinkable. It was his castle, his land; he felt himself to be unassailable.[1] A letter of 1917 from Milly to Sydney indicates that she took a more realistic view:

> When I tell you that my husband is a very militant Orangeman, and has a big Lodge here, the Leap Loyal Independents, I shall not

1 'My father simply could not imagine that anything could happen to Leap.' Diana, in a recorded conversation with the late Richard Dill.

need to explain that 'Nationalist' of any kind is not persona grata...

She goes on to speak of whether, 'in the *very possible* event of a much more widespread and better organised Rising we should be safe here...' adding: 'When one thinks of the past history of the Distressful Country it is a marvel that now the Protestant Ascendancy is on its last legs the members of the Older Church do *not* try to give us a taste of what our lot gave them for centuries.' Her husband would have been outraged, had he known that Milly voiced such an opinion. She was not expected to have opinions, let alone express them.

Instances of Jonathan Darby's perceived shortcomings are recorded, not wholly without affection, in the reminiscences of Michael Walsh, a one-time Leap employee and subsequently the local postman. Even making allowances for the distortion of memory due to old age, these recorded recollections of local happenings up to and including the castle's burning, made in 1980 by Mr Delaney for the Irish Folklore Association and transcribed by him verbatim under the overall title of 'The Dead Coach', have an air of authenticity about them as well as a liveliness and perspicacity that make them hard to put down. Fed as I have been on tales of Leap as seen by the inhabitants of the castle, this picture of life from outside the walls gives depth to that two-dimensional view. The scope of Mr Walsh's memoirs extends beyond the precincts of the Leap community, but it is from this small area that I shall quote instances that shed a revealing light both on the state of affairs at Leap from an employee's point of view and, later, on the burning of the castle.

Many of these anecdotes of life under the Darbys are classic tales of man outwitting master. One such recalls an occasion when Leap timber was cut on a certain dark night for hurling sticks by local enthusiasts for the sport [2] and the theft discovered by my grandfather. 'Well, 'e was ragin'!' says Mr Walsh, but the culprits talked their way out of trouble. Another tale tells of Jonathan erecting a wall to stop the Catholic priest crossing his land, and posting the local policeman to guard it. The policeman, it seems, was on the side of the priest, ensuring his future safe passage through a discreet hole in the wall, undiscovered by Jonathan. There are several other instances of this cat-and-mouse game played between landlord and tenants, with no real ill will on either side. In fact, Michael Walsh goes out of his way to relate instances of my

2 An Irish national game, played with wooden blocks or 'hurls'.

grandfather's generosity, the most notable being his open-handed support of the new Catholic church under construction at Clareen, not far from Leap. Jonathan evidently did not allow his dislike for a certain trespassing priest to prevent his support for the church the priest represented. 'Darby was a good sort' is Michael Walsh's declared verdict. Not that that counted for anything when the order came to burn him and his family out.

Mr Walsh's one-time membership of the IRA does not distinguish him from a number of others in the vicinity who felt oppressed by the powerful landlords and infused with a renewed sense of their Irish identity, the seeds of which had been sown by the Gaelic Revival movement as far back as the 1880s, reawakening a sense of cultural heritage. Subsequently, the Gaelic League was founded in 1894 to promote the regeneration of the Irish language. All this gathered momentum over the years, filtering down through the ranks of the intelligentsia to ordinary men and women, further activating their sense of oppression with the high-octane fuel of nationalism. Moreover, the Land Wars won for the Irish by Parnell had, after his untimely death in 1891, given many of the previously landless Irish holdings of their own. These became a new class of semi-prosperous small farmers, and the period of political stagnation that followed served to heighten the frustration of those not in a position to obtain land for themselves. This all came to a head at the time of the Easter Rising in 1916 and erupted again in the Civil War of 1922–3. More land would only be available by getting rid of landowners like Jonathan Darby and it was a small step in the reasoning processes of the landless to assume that the land would then be theirs for the taking. Lust by the Irish for Irish soil was the prime motive for the wanton destruction of Leap, and in the last analysis we can discount my grandfather's unpopularity as a reason for ruining him.

In the section of 'The Dead Coach' memoirs entitled 'Burning of Leap in 1922', Mr Walsh starts with the allegation that he had twice saved my grandfather's life but was reluctant to speak further about it. It is here that he declares his membership of the IRA, 'time of the Tans'.[3] This motley collection of British ex-servicemen and former inmates of Manchester gaol, ill-disciplined and often wantonly destructive, were burning down all Sinn Féiners' houses in the vicinity, and

3 The 'Black and Tans', or British Army Auxiliaries, brought in to reinforce the Irish Constabulary when the Anglo-Irish civil war broke out in 1916. So called because of their half-military, half-constabulary garb, they were named after a famous pack of foxhounds.

provoked a counter-offensive by locals like Michael Walsh. These protesters (the Irregulars) retaliated by attacking in Walsh's own words, 'the likes of Darby' who were 'justices of the peace and magistrates and all that'. Walsh and his fellow IRA men threatened that 'all their castles would be burned out if the Tans burned any more Sinn Féin houses. Only for that, the Sinn Féiners' houses would be all burned down.'

It was at this time that Leap was under constant threat, and almost certainly when Mr Walsh allegedly intervened to protect the life of the very man he was shortly to help to ruin. By March of 1922 the Darby family had left Leap, for their own safety. Rumours then became rife.

A misunderstanding regarding Jonathan Darby's intentions for the future of the castle and estate also emerges from Michael Walsh's memories. I shall quote the passage in full, with the tape recordist's punctuation and clarifying additions, for the description brings to life the events that led to Leap's burning, even though we must allow for some confusion over the sequence of events. Michael Walsh explains that one evening after the fire he was 'praisin'' Jonathan Darby to his Protestant friend Mr Short.

> 'What,' says he, 'did ye burn 'im for, then?'
>
> 'It wasn't us burned 'im, it was *ye* burned 'im. The bloody aul Bill Cosgrave[4] and his Free State Government burned 'im!'
>
> 'How d'ye make that out? They [the Free State troops] were fightin' for law and order!'
>
> 'They were fightin'' says I, 'for the Divil! They were fightin' for whatever England tauld them to fight for!'
>
> 'And what have they got to do with it? Wasn't it ye that burned it?'
>
> 'Well, says I, 'the Free State come in and they measured it [i.e. the Castle] an' looked at it an' they were going to fortify it with a big Free State Army an' it id be impossible to penetrate it. An then they'd operate all around about it with their army, but our I O's [intelligence officers] found it out and they reported it... an' they came up and burnt it to the ground.'

This, then, was one fear felt by the local resistance movement. It may well have gained credence in that Birr Castle did become a temporary barracks at that time. A further cause for alarm, according to Michael

4 William Cosgrove (1880–1965), chairman of the Provisional Government April 1919–September 1922 and subsequently president of the executive council of the Free State.

Walsh, was a rumour that, since all the estate workers had been dismissed except for the gardener and a few farm hands, it was clear that the castle was to be put up for sale, so that tenants would be put out. In truth, the majority of the farm hands and all the other servants had been laid off on account of the Darby family's enforced flight after sixteen break-ins and several threatening letters in March 1922.[5]

The clear implication is that the locals, whether employees, tenants or both, albeit greedy for the land, acted when they did in fear both of Free State domination based on the castle itself, and of summary eviction. This would have been as great an anxiety to the Protestant tenants as to the far fewer Catholic ones, which may account for why no one subsequently helped to put the fire out. The two fears were grounded in hearsay but no less potent for that. As it was, my grandfather stated at the hearing at Roscommon in 1922 that he never had any intention of selling up, and indeed it is unthinkable that he of all people would have considered such action. As to the rumour that the Free State Army was to garrison the place, I can find no record of any such plan. It does, however seem probable that once my grandparents had been driven out of their home, communication beween them and the people on the estate became virtually non-existent. Fears that might have been assuaged were left to proliferate. Warnings to Grandfather, even if given, would have fallen on deaf ears. Canute-like, Jonathan seems to have believed that the rising tide of nationalism would somehow circumvent the Darbys of Leap.

Michael Walsh's account of the actual burning is inaccurate in one or two respects. He states that after the Free State Army's alleged survey of the castle and grounds with a view to occupation, the local IRA, which, as he said earlier, included himself and others on the estate, 'came up an' burnt it to the ground'.

In Michael's recollection, the burning did not take place on two consecutive nights, which was in fact the case. He speaks of a first attempt, on the night of 22 July, to burn the south wing, and of the efforts of some neighbours, both Protestants and Catholics, to put the fire out. This, he says, they managed to do, having cut a beam down to prevent the spread of fire to the rest of the building. The latter assertion is in contradiction to the evidence given later at the hearing, when it is claimed by Mr Dawkins, the steward, that he and his wife took this action after the first fire on 29 July. The narrative continues with an account of a meeting of the local branch of the IRA in the following

5 Reported by Jonathan Darby at Tullamore Quarter Sessions, June 1924.

week when Michael Walsh and his companions were 'ordered to go look at it on Thursday to try would we have to go set fire to the right wing again'. It seems that while the meetings and the delegation of Michael Walsh and his companion as observers did take place, he made a mistake over the date of the first fire – he was, after all, recalling events of nearly sixty years before. He goes on to admit that on that fateful night he and his companions soon abandoned their role as observers and joined the vandals, and the eyewitness description that follows is so vivid that I shall quote it in full:

> We gathered aul planks an' timber an' everything an' we flung it in. We said we'd have it to say *we* gave great help to burn down the castle... But aye! There was Dawkins. He was the chief manager, an' there was a fella the name o' Nee... a gamekeeper.[6] They were employed on the estate. All the others was sacked. Then there did some Unionists from way down at our back come, and they all lookin' (at the ruin) an' they said wasn't it a pity! 'It'll bring the curse o' God almighty on our own, burnin' a fine buildin' like that...'

The next day, and the day following, the looters arrived, many of them local people. Michael Walsh's account continues:

> Nee, the gamekeeper, an' Dawkins, an' the wife...had a whole lot of stuff dragged out on the lawn... in front o' the house, armchairs, tables, bedclothes, shirts, books, an' anythin' an' everythin'. The whole place was full. Ye'd think there was goin' to be a great big auction. But there was women an' childer lootin' an' we knew some o' them but some... we didn't know. And they didn't know but we were looters, too... But there was an' aul' man and woman...an they had an ass and car, said 'Young fellas! Young fellas! Give us a lift with this!' Well, there was a table... about four feet square... 'Christ!' says I, 'This must be an iron table or something!' I suppose it was mahogany. But we lifted it. We said: 'The best way ye'd put that, throw it on its back in the ass's car an' fling all ye can on the top of it an'get off ou' o' this as as quick as ye can!'
>
> We were both young, an' we stood like this, lookin' up at the flames. An' there'd be calmness. Suddenly there'd be a gust o' wind, an' black smoke an' flames an' sparks id go up into th'air.

6 Nee does not feature in any of the other accounts.

> An then, a floor'd collapse, a great big floor. An' then it'd be burnt down, an' suddenly it 'd collapse down onto the next floor and there'd be explosions. We thought it could be heard in Birr. Well, we stood silently, side by side, watchin'.

That Michael Walsh should have retained this picture in his mind for all those years and that Mr Delaney should have recorded it for posterity is a rare achievement on both counts. Shocking, tragic, infinitely sad, the picture has the vivid quality of something deeply felt and undimmed by time. Behind it, almost by mistake, we see the spectacle of two grimy figures, scarcely more than boys, elated yet horrified. Michael Walsh neither justifies nor excuses his part in that act of vandalism. He was courageous to tell of it.

Michael's account of the burning of Leap has the ring of truth about it, even though he did get some of the details wrong. The brief account given on the insurance claim form encapsulates in outline the immediate circumstances that led to the place being broken into and destroyed and is probably accurate:

> Following some labour dispute which applicant had he and his family were compelled to leave this country. The Castle and Premises were being looked after by an Employee of his who resided therein. On date in question a number of Armed Raiders came to the Castle and demanded the keys, but as these were not forthcoming they affected an entrance by breaking in the doors…

Having done so, the intruders are believed to have then made their way to Grandfather's cellars, where they got well and truly drunk before planting bombs and dynamite and setting fire to the castle.

As soon as the events of those two days and nights became known, further dramatic accounts of the burning were reported by several journalists, and printed in many of the local and national newspapers as well as in the English press. The *Yorkshire Post* ran an article that began: 'The passing of an historic mansion is always a matter for regret, but the burning of Leap Castle, a famous link with the past, dear alike to archeologists and antiquaries as well as to students of psychical research, has provoked widespread condemnation and sorrow.' An account of the history of the castle continues:

> When, with unprovoked malice, the Republicans set fire to it, the owners were away, but efforts were made by the servants to rescue some of the priceless furniture from the flames. The 'saviours of

Ireland', however, were determined to do their work thoroughly. They came back from Roscrea the next morning, accompanied by their colleagues, the looters; the latter seized everything portable they could lay their hands on, and then the castle was fired again. Only the burnt out walls remain.

An eloquent and heartfelt observation that follows mirrors the reaction to the burning of Leap felt by all civilised people who were not in one degree or another Irish freedom fighters. The writer expresses the hope that his article on the castle will 'bring home to peaceful Englanders the agony and martyrdom which Irish loyalists, helpless, defenceless, unarmed and without protection, are enduring at the hands of de Valera and his satellites'.

Further details are furnished by a reporter from the *Midland Tribune* on 5 August 1922.This account mentions that 'the workmen had saved a quantity of the furniture and stored it in one of the out-houses, which was broken into and looted the following night'. This is a particularly nasty twist in the story; these people were not caught up in the horrible drama of the initial fire; they were common thieves.

Of all the accounts of the burning, it is my grandmother's letter to her friend Sydney Carroll that is the most heartrending. She writes from my parents' home in England, on Monday 7 August:

> The details of the destruction of Leap have now reached me. On Sunday night before last the Flying Column of one or other I.R.A – as I told you it is often impossible to tell t'other from which, arrived at 2 a.m. and by means of 30 bombs and 20 cases of petrol began the work. Sunday and Monday saw endless crowds of donkey and horse carts coming and going, looting all worth taking. Monday night saw the return of the incendiaries with more bombs for any crumbling walls, more petrol to pour over the mass of ruins. On Thursday via Dublin as the roads are impassable my husband found a still smouldering mass of charred stones to mark the site of the home of your mutual ancestors, and the looting so complete that even poultry and turf gone. He is back safe with daughter Cis. Beyond the few clothes we took when we fled to Doory[7] all our personal property went, all land and estate papers gone between the Record etc in the Four Courts, and now our own copies in Milner safe in my husband's office roasted ashes.

7 The home of the Minchins, whence Jonathan and Milly had gone on 25 March.

This account is written directly after the event, and reveals Milly's fortitude. Still in shock, she may later have had a bad reaction, but, even if she did, this was someone who would have put a brave face on it when out in the world. Her letter to Sydney Carroll continues:

> … Absolutely no home to go to if 'times' grow safer, no stock, no farming machines, barns, stables, no anything left! We are Irish so you won't be surprised to hear that Di and her Eddie and her sister Florrie[8] all go over to Dublin for the Horse Show next week where daughter Cis and her Ted meet them, Cis riding her hunters in the jumping competition…
>
> Yours still smiling, MILDRED H. G. DARBY

In fact, not quite everything in the castle was either burnt or looted. The Dawkinses managed to hide various things from the south wing, including some of the books, silver and priceless mirrors, in the bushes, where they lay undiscovered until rescued and stored at neighbouring Anglo-Irish houses.

It was two long years before the case of the burning of Leap Castle came up before the local magistrates. Burnings had been legion in the vicinity in the period of unleashed fury and near anarchy that preceded the ceasefire on 30 April 1923, and the list of complainants was a correspondingly long one. However, on 5 June 1924, the *Midland Tribune* reported on the hearing at Birr Quarter Sessions with regard to claims for compensation put forward by my grandfather. By this time a clear and full account of what happened on the two fateful nights of Sunday and Monday the 30 and 31 July two years previously had been compiled, and witnesses gave detailed evidence under oath. The first to be called was Mr Dawkins, and the newspaper account reads as follows:

> The applicant's steward and gardener, Richard Dawkins, who came from England to give evidence, said he had been employed by Mr. Darby in July 1922, and on the 29th of that month he and his wife were living in a house at the Castle.[9] On that date, a Sunday, a knock came on the door at 2.20 in the morning. Witness asked what was wanted and men outside said they wanted a night's lodging and told witness to open the door. Witness went down and opened the door and immediately found himself confronted with a revolver. There was a number of men there, and

8 Patricia.

9 Evidently, the Dawkinses were in residence in servants' quarters attached to the castle.

when asked what they wanted they said that they were going to burn the Castle. Witness asked to be given time to get out his wife and was given twenty minutes to clear out. The men then went and poured petrol all over the place, witness being kept outside from 2.20 until 4.30 a.m. He saw eleven men altogether, each of whom carried a tin of petrol. They were armed; some were dressed in trench coats and others in civilian clothes, with bandoliers. [This report omits to mention that the castle was then set alight.] On Monday morning they came back again and knocked at the gate lodge, to which the witness had gone to live, and asked for paraffin oil. Witness said he had no oil... and they went off stating that they would get it elsewhere. Later, when witness went to the castle at 2.40 a.m. he found that the castle was all burned. There had been two distinct fires. After the fire on Monday morning there was nothing intact. The servants had left, and were not there when the fire occurred. After the first fire...they were able to save some of the furniture, but after the second fire they were unable to save anything.

Cross-examined by Mr. Rogers, witness said he was kept outside for a couple of hours during which the raiders were sprinkling petrol and burning the place. Witness saw them breaking furniture in that part of the building known as the small hall. They left at 4.40 a.m. telling witness not to stir out of the place where he stood. After the first fire the castle was intact but it was almost completely destroyed after the second fire. On Monday morning between 10 and 11 o'clock witness went to Roscrea and reported what had occurred... Witness reported the matter to the Free State forces in Roscrea, but no steps were taken with a view to saving the building or putting out the fire... Witness did not go to Roscrea for assistance on Sunday as he was trying to save some of the furniture. He asked for help but the people who were asked to assist witness only laughed at him. Another reason why witness did not go to Roscrea ... was that he was trying to cut the gallery down ... to save one part of the building.[10] He succeeded in doing this, and so prevented one side of the castle from being burned. In reply to His Honour, witness said that no one offered to help him in his efforts to save the building... A great many people came to see the place while the fire was in progress but nobody gave any assistance... Further cross-examined, ... witness said the gallery

10 This is the 'beam' referred to by Michael Walsh in his recollections.

> divided the buildings into two portions and only for the fire on Monday morning one portion of the castle would have been intact... He could not save the valuable pictures because they were in that part of the building that was on fire. The only assistance witness got was from his wife...
>
> Replying to Mr. Rogers, Mr. Dawkins said that Mr. Darby ceased to reside in Leap Castle in March 1922. Previous to that the servants were all paid off... Afterwards Mr. Darby returned to the castle from time to time. When the servants were paid off and Mr. Darby left, none of the furniture was removed.

The family accounts of the burning were doubtless drawn from Mr Dawkins and from others on the spot and amplified by this later evidence. They include the macabre incident, not mentioned by the press, of the drunken incendiaries bursting into the dining room, tearing down the portraits of the three Darby warriors and slashing their faces with knives before setting the place alight and hurling the wrecked pictures into the flames. Jonathan Darby's plate-smashing tantrum of a few years previously seems positively restrained beside this act of savagery, enacted on the premises of Leap, in that very same room. It is now a pile of rubble.

A year later, on 14 February 1925, the *Midland Tribune* reported upon the case for reparations at the Quarter Sessions at Tullamore, presided over by a High Court Judge. Many Irish newspapers carried an account of this report, with only minor differences; by then it had become something of a *cause célèbre*. There had already been much discussion in previous court hearings both on what Jonathan Darby might claim and on his possible plans for the future use of the property, which need not concern us here. After a lengthy recapitulation of the circumstances that had occasioned the inquiry, in which my grandfather pleaded his own case most eloquently, the decision on the Leap Castle burning application was announced. The *Midland Tribune* tells us that Jonathan Darby was awarded £3,050 for the contents and £3,900 for the loss of the castle itself. More would have been given (£5,100) had there been an intention to restore the ruined parts, but: 'Witness would not re-build the castle as his heart was not in the place now.'

Having originally sued for £35,000,[11] Jonathan Darby was bitterly disappointed. He never again lived on the soil of his forefathers, and the land was bought by compulsory acquisition following the Land Act

11 *The Midland Tribune*, 19 August 1922.

of 1923, and sold on to the tenant farmers. According to the Land Commission records, 3,288 acres changed hands, and Grandfather was paid approximately £31,546 in Land Bonds, which were paid out at 4.5% per year.[12] Nothing remained but the few acres that surround the castle to this day.

Haunted as I am by the destruction of Leap, I have seen enough in my lifetime of the warping and festering effect that fear, a sense of injustice and whipped-up nationalistic fervour can have on the minds and actions of 'ordinary' individuals to understand how such people could have caused so cruel a catastrophe; have so wounded a family whose children they probably knew by their Christian names, whose womenfolk had, if reports are to be believed, long regarded it as their duty to alleviate suffering among those for whom fate had made them responsible. I *can* imagine hurling paraffin into a cherished space like a child's playroom or a mother's boudoir, inflamed by indignation that masked a surge of elation at doing down the privileged. I *can* imagine joining in the cries and whoops of triumph as I grabbed the cherished artefacts of others and smashed what I could not use. A country's ruthless pursuit of its racial identity, often taking far more horrifying forms than was the case in Ireland, is usually the result of a history of oppression and deprivation. Those of us born into happier circumstances have never been tempted to sip from this poisoned chalice.

12 I am indebted to Noel Guerin for this information.

9
After the Burning

As I come to consider the after-effects of the burning, some of them are within the bounds of my comprehension, some are not. I can envisage only to a small extent the sense of total desolation that must have assailed my grandmother in the wake of the destruction. Apart from the sacking of her home and its contents, the catalogue of her personal losses in the inventory of possessions for which reimbursement was to be sought is poignant beyond words. Leaving aside the expected complement of serviceable tweeds, stout shoes and stockings, riding-habits, furs and waterproof garments of several varieties, the list includes all her pretty petticoats and chemises, her chiffon blouses and nightgowns, and her formal attire such as her 'Parisian Court Dress and Train', her three 'beaded and spangled Evening Dresses', her opera cloak, even her Brussels lace wedding veil, 'the property of her Great Grandmother'. Most of her jewellery, locked in the melted safe, also went. How could she have left so much behind? Did they move out in a great hurry? A letter to Sydney Carroll, dated 7 August, speaks of 'When we fled in the car to Doory'[1] and another mentions 'an anonymous threatening letter', which may have expedited their departure, but it still seems odd that between their flight in March and the burning at the end of July nothing further was done to save anything.

The loss of her beautiful clothes and treasured jewels must have caused my grandmother to feel bereft in a way that those of us who set store by such things (most women, that is) can relate to, with sorrow and sympathy. Her possessions were part of her identity – the identity that her husband had tried so hard to crush. Novelist that she was, I expect Milly saw in her mind's eye and with her customary irony her neighbours strutting about in their looted finery. But here my empathy with Milly's loss fails. As a lover of creative writing, I do not think I can begin to conceive of my grandmother's reaction to the destruction of all her unpublished manuscripts. That is akin to losing your life-blood.

1 The home of her son-in-law and daughter, Edward and Cecily Minchin.

The list is long, and includes 'a drawer full of...short stories and articles, Cinema rights, publishers' agreements, etc. etc. for last 30 years, impossible to replace...', and a 'Drawer with over 150 printed short stories and articles on which the republication, book form and Cinema rights were retained by the author...'. The list continues with further drawers containing numerous unpublished stories and plays, as well as two completed novels not yet submitted for publication. That her husband had forbidden her to publish any further work some thirteen years previously seems not to have extinguished her output – that large body of work could not possibly have all been completed before the prohibition.

'Ladybird, Ladybird, fly away home, your house is on fire and your children all gone' ran the nursery rhyme of my childhood. Naturally, Granny was the ladybird in my mind and I was pleased her children were not all gone. Yet I now see that, having left home, in a sense they *were* all gone – even teenage Patricia was away at school in England. Latterly, I have realised that the rhyme went on being half true, for it continues 'All but one, and her name is Anne, and she hid under the frying pan'. Milly's remaining child, named not Anne but Andrew Merry, was indeed in the house on fire, but in the absence of an adjacent frying pan went up in flames. This was akin to the death of a second child, the offspring of her mind, of her whole creative being. By comparison, the loss of those little chemises, those grand outfits, those jewels, was as nothing. I would not presume to imagine that I could understand how Milly felt.

What of Grandfather's suffering? To be sure, he missed his guns and rods, his five pairs of top boots, his hunting coats and dress suits, to name but a few of his listed possessions, and he must have mourned the destruction of his entire cellar, of which seventeen dozen bottles of vintage port was but one item among many. But what of losing his castle, his garden, his stables, his farm buildings, his horses, his prized herd and all the priceless ancestral possessions that he held in trust for future generations? Richard White-Spunner, the boy whom Jonathan befriended and taught country skills, recalls that when, years later, Jonathan spent much of his time at Milltown Park with Richard's widowed Aunt Florence, the three of them would stroll together through the Italian garden at Milltown, with Grandfather calling to mind, one at a time, every prized heirloom that he had loved and lost.

Could anything be worse for Jonathan Darby than this? One thing only, and it was much, much worse. It was his identity as a person who mattered, in a fixed order of things, that was the the most agonising loss of all. I am reminded of Othello. Bereft of his office as a great general in the service of his country, his assertion that 'Othello's occupation's gone' is a profound moment in the drama. That was the real tragedy for Jonathan Charles Darby of The Leap. His occupation was gone. Bred to administer the land of his fathers[2] he was a man without inner resources, a man who, still full of fury, became a pastiche of what he had been, yet retaining, to his great credit, courage and dignity. That telling phrase, reported at the Tullamore Quarter Sessions in February 1925, 'Witness would not re-build the castle, as his heart was not in the place now', bears repetition here. Observe Jonathan's face, a few months later, at what should have been a happy occasion, Patricia's wedding ceremony. It is the face of a man who has, for the time being, lost heart about everything.

Jonathan and Milly continued to live on in Ireland after the burning. With the money that he eventually received as compensation, together with the proceeds from the compulsory sale to the Free State government of most of the land he still owned, a large bungalow was built for them on Lough Derg, at Barrack Bay, Dromineer, which remained their home until my grandmother's death in 1932. Milly's letters to my mother and to Patricia reveal that the two of them were no happier there than they had been at Leap, and she spent a lot of time visiting her relations overseas. Patricia, married to a serving officer in the Navy and the mother of two children, was usually stationed abroad. Grandfather was also often away from home, staying with Florence White-Spunner at Milltown Park. Although the *status quo* was preserved by the sharing of a house, Jonathan and Milly were now as distant as it was possible for a married couple to be, while fiercely denying, in deference to the social conventions of the time, that their marriage was anything out of the ordinary. And yet, almost in spite of themselves they were probably yoked together by the enormity of their loss. In the last resort they had that one agony in common, until my grandmother's death from pneumonia, accelerated, as I have said, by the chain of Turkish cigarettes. She died on 5 January 1932, aged sixty-two, just under ten years after the burning.

I have a copy of Milly's cremation service, (yet more fire) and wonder who chose Psalm xxxix. 'Dixi Custodiam'. I cannot believe that no one was aware of the *double entendre* implicit in the opening verses:

2 When he inherited, Jonathan owned 4,376 acres, mostly tenanted.

> I said, I will take heed of my ways: that I offend not with my tongue.
>
> I will keep my mouth as it were with a bridle: while the ungodly is in my sight.
>
> I kept my tongue and spake nothing: I kept silence, even from good words; but it was pain and grief to me.
>
> My heart was hot within me, and while I was thus musing the fire kindled....

'I kept my tongue and spake nothing': how often must Milly have had to resort to this tactic!

In one of her letters to my mother after my parents' marriage, my grandmother, evidently responding to a *cri de coeur* from her daughter, replies as follows: 'Keep on old girl and remember as long as YOU don't yield to the temptation to retaliate in words YOU are the injured one and the knowledge of this must be a well deserved punishment to a GENTLEMAN...'.

I wish that her advice had been less negative, less bitter, but there speaks one who had been trapped in an unhappy marriage for years and clearly used a pregnant silence as a weapon in what seems to have been a permanent battle of wills. That she did not always follow her own counsel is evident from the many descriptions by our elders of blood rows ringing through the castle. Perhaps it was because of these that noisy marital battles were the norm with the next generation. Leap in its last years was a scene of warfare (albeit of a domestic kind) as it had so often been in days of old, before the Darbys came. The habit of discord remained with the two of them for the rest of their married life.

After Granny died, Jonathan retired to a bungalow at Howth, on the outskirts of Dublin. A photograph taken around that time reveals him as he was, an old gentleman, impeccably turned out, pictured with a map of Ireland and a portrait of his favourite dog on the wall behind him and his radio beside him. He had not retreated into the past; he listened to every news bulletin with alert interest. His face says the rest: I am bloody but unbowed.

At this time, my grandfather took to visiting his old friend Florence White-Spunner with increasing frequency. Perhaps Florence was his only confidante after the burning, which was very hard on my grandmother as her letters to her daughters testify.[3] Florence's husband Harry

3 These are full of instances of his aloofness, intractability and overbearing ways, and of innuendoes about Florence.

had died in a shooting accident – his gun went off as he was riding his mule – and after his death she ran the estate. She too rode a mule, which was quite eccentric behaviour even in the Ireland of those days, and she was renowned for her strong Christian Scientist views. Whether Jonathan Darby shared those views I do not know, but it seems likely that he did, since he was the parent who most influenced my mother, and she was extremely bracing about infirmities, dismissing all but near total incapacity as self-indulgent nonsense. I don't, however, recall her inviting God to intervene: her own censure was usually enough to get us going.

Richard White-Spunner now lives with his wife Janet at beautiful Milltown Park. He had a warm regard for his Aunt Florence, and recalls the day that the IRA called at the house when she was there alone, tied her to the knob of the front door and dug a pit in the drive in front of her which they told her was to be her grave. They went away, leaving Florence tied up, and never returned.

It is clear from my grandmother's unhappy letters to her daughters in the years following the burning that she regarded Florence as more than a friend to Jonathan, but Richard dismisses this as nonsense on a number of counts, and I accept his verdict. That Jonathan did not care what his wife thought is extremely likely, and because of this Milly may have been caused a great deal of unnecessary grief. It is understandable that after her death Jonathan turned in his solitude to his old widowed friend for companionship; there was probably no more to the situation than that, either then or earlier. In Richard's own words: 'The servants would never have stood for it': a reflection on the stern Protestant morality that would have prevailed in such households.

A little before the outbreak of war in 1939, my grandfather went to live with my Aunt Cis and her second husband, Uncle Bob Smyth, at Gaybrook, near Mullingar, where I had twice spent a happy part of my summer holidays from school. I remember Grandfather in those days, on my last visit, with less terror than when I was small. We children, Anne, Robert and I, kept out of his way, but I recall his holding forth endlessly at meals on various topics of the day, in the high Darby male voice that was so much at odds with their manliness. At other times he would fall silent, drumming on the smooth dining-room table with his long, strong fingers, making tiny pits in the surface where his fingernails struck it. My aunt was almost maniacally houseproud but she never batted an eyelid when this was happening. She was a kind person. My step-cousin Robert recalls that even at the height of wartime privation

Grandfather was given a nightly whiskey and soda, which Robert and Anne thought was grossly unfair to their father, who was more than partial to whiskey himself and not allowed it. Aunt Cis clearly considered that her father had suffered enough hardship in his long life and deserved this small comfort. I hope he found contentment, if not happiness, with that delightful family, in surroundings that were unusually charming and beautiful, even by Irish country house standards. I cherish the memory of Gaybrook.

I do not know if Jonathan ever visited Leap in his last years. He died at Gaybrook on 22 March 1943 aged eighty-seven, while on his daily walk with Bridget, an old family retainer who had stayed on in his service after Milly's death. According to Robert, he just sat down by the side of the drive, in his long grey overcoat and his trilby hat, and never got up again. Robert, exhibiting already the lawyer's dispassionate scrutiny of events, found it curious that the Gaybrook butler described this bizarre episode as 'a beautiful death'. It was a merciful one, to be sure, for an old man who may have had a few things on his conscience. Perhaps that was what the butler meant.

Grandfather's remains lie in the family vault in Aghancon churchyard, a few yards from the church where he had read the lesson weekly and bellowed at the village boys for cracking nuts during the sermon, as Milly relates in a letter to Sydney.[4] Jonathan must have seemed a fair imitation of wrathful Yahweh to them. At the time of his burial, there would have been many people in the vicinity who had known him, perhaps some of them already regretting their part in his downfall while welcoming the new freedoms and relative prosperity. It was to be the very last occasion that the Darbys of Leap assembled at their erstwhile village church. There is, understandably, no memorial to Grandfather inside the prim little building. With the passing of Jonathan Charles Darby, a whole strand of local history was finally cut out of the fabric. The Darbys were gone for good.

4 This incident also features in her novel *The Green Country* (Grant Richards, 1902), p. 12.

10
The Rescuers

On the death of my grandfather in 1942 Leap in its ruined state was inherited by his son, Horatio Darby, my uncle Boysie. Horatio deeded it to Sam Spencer, who had been a faithful employee of the Darbys and had kept an eye on the place after the burning for many years. The ballroom, outbuildings and some land had been sold to the Standish family in the mid 1920s. They made the ballroom into a house and still farm the land. Leap itself underwent several vicissitudes[1] before it began to be rescued from dereliction, after more than half a century as an empty ruin.

The first rescuer was Peter Bartlett, a young Australian. I wish I had known him, partly because those people I have met who did know him have all said how glad they were to have done so. My other reason is perhaps more cogent: I feel he was a kindred spirit, because of an extraordinarily kind and imaginative thing that his sister Betty Foster did when I wrote to her to ask her permission to dedicate this book to him as well as to Seán Ryan. She sent me, amongst much valuable information about her brother, a sale catalogue of his rare books. Whenever I am at the house of a stranger I have an irresistible compulsion to look at that person's bookshelves; you can tell, almost at once, far more about them than you would learn in hours of conversation.

Peter's book-list reveals a man of wide culture and a multiplicity of literary and aesthetic tastes. Aeschylus and Aristophanes, amongst the As, are cheek by jowl with Auden, African Stone Sculpture and Architecture, while a random glance at the Bs gives us Francis Bacon, Brigid Brophy, Boer War, [Isaiah] Berlin, James Baldwin, volumes galore of Baedekker; Botany, Bunyan, Blunden; I could go through the alphabet with page after page of reading matter on almost every subject within a civilised context that you could think of. The photographs Betty sent, too, reflect this impression: he looks like a bright, noble bird in one, while in the other I see a gentle, humorous philosopher. In both, there is an engaging hint of quirkiness. Everyone says what fun he was, and I

1 See Appendix 6.

would guess he carried his erudition lightly, like a knapsack, as he made his way to the destination of the moment.

What's in a name? For Peter, in this case, a profound sense of personal association. His mother was descended from the O'Bannons, of the very same clan as those brothers who allegedly jumped from the top of Leap's battlements to settle the question of which of them should own it, causing it to be known thereafter as Lemevannon, or O'Bannon's Leap. Peter's great-grandmother on his mother's side came from Clonmel, near Cork, and left Ireland following the Potato Famine in 1850, returning later to marry a Mr Lonegan. It was one of their three daughters who emigrated to Australia in the 1880s and married Henry Banon, a mining engineer in Kalgoorlie, Western Australia. Many of Henry's O'Bannon forebears, like the O'Carrolls themselves, had been forced to leave their native land in Cromwellian or Williamite times. One branch settled in France and became cheese-makers for a living (a sheep's milk cheese named 'Banon' is still to be had in the village of that name in southern France), while another descendant became Regent of Parma. An earlier ancestor of Peter's was the abbot of Roscrea monastery; he died in 1128. Peter also had several recent Irish connections amongst the landed nobility so that he must have felt European and, more specifically, Irish, as well as Australian – a mixed heritage of considerable interest. All this, and much more, is graphically summed up by Betty, who writes:

> What does all this mean to Leap? Peter was a mixture of English, Irish, Scottish...Catholic and Protestant, Lord, Carpenter and Convict. He was an educated man of the world, Historian and Playwright and Thespian. Who better to appreciate and restore Leap?

In 1974 Peter, who was also an ex-diplomat, arrived at Leap from Australia in the course of a holiday spent in discovering the area where his ancestors had lived. Finding that the castle was up for sale and concluding that this was a coincidence too potent to ignore, he abandoned himself to the love of it and bought it. Possessed as he was of a romantic as well as an imaginative and resourceful nature, he set about restoring the ruined shell with a drive and enthusiasm that amazed the neighbours. His charm and ease of manner quickly won him a host of friends as well as a number of useful contacts who, fired by his zeal and capacity for hard work, helped him to put his plans into effect. Betty writes: 'The happiest time of his life was rebuilding the gate lodge and tackling the castle with Joe Sullivan.'[2] This is borne out by a charming letter that Peter wrote in 1988 to my Aunt Patricia, about to visit Ireland from British Columbia in her eighties, in which he says: 'It would be a great pleasure to show you the work that has been done on your old home. I am so much enjoying living here.' My aunt was delighted, and I believe that a happy encounter ensued.

Leap was by no means Peter Bartlett's sole consuming project; he was too much of a polymath to limit himself in that way, but he did intend that Leap should be in some sense both a centre from which artistic enterprises could evolve and a catalyst for his own creative energies. Since those of us who set store by such things have observed that the castle stands on an 'energy point'caused by the crossing of two 'ley lines', I believe that it could all have happened more easily than might be imagined. Called 'dragon lines' by the Chinese, ley lines are earth energies, discernible to primitive man and channelled in prehistoric times into specific directions; in Britain by aligned temples and megalithic monuments. Ley lines (so named by the late Alfred Watkins) serve to energise routes and destinations, and such actions, good or otherwise, as may take place within their areas. They are easily identified today by 'sensitives', even without dowsing equipment. Where ley lines cross, the spot is doubly empowered, and human thought or action in that place is liable to have a magnified effect. I have no doubt that Peter, equipped as he was to achieve his aims even without such outside help, would have made something remarkable of the restored Leap; enabling it to become both a home and a centre of entertainment on a broad front, and, perhaps most important of all, a venue for the exchange of ideas, as a kind of by-product of all the rest.

Although I never knew Peter Bartlett, it is clear that he was someone with an enormous and infectious enjoyment of life. At the party he gave at Leap in celebration of his fortieth birthday, Betty tells me that he put a lighted candle in every window and invited all the people he had met in the last month, as well as friends and relations from all over the world. This was a true festival, the birthday of a man 'returned to his roots' as Betty puts it, with spirits human, disembodied and bottled combining to create the merriest of galas. Leap, which had long slumbered fitfully in humiliation, rage and sorrow, had, because of Peter, begun its gradual awakening into joy and peace. Little did most of the guests know that this event was to be one of hail and farewell.

2 Joe is a skilled builder and became a great friend of Peter.

Peter died in Australia the following year, on 10 June 1989. In her obituary of him, published in the *Tribune* on 24 June Alison Rosse, a devoted friend, says of him:

> His enthusiasm carried all before it, and the most impossible tasks were accomplished as when, with only one helper, huge 30 ft. beams were pulled into place in some magic way to make a floor....

This is a vivid metaphor of Peter's life. He was above all a man who made things happen; good things, that enriched the world he lived in. I, knowing Peter only by repute, am amongst those who give thanks for his life.

A simple memorial service was held for Peter Bartlett in the hall at Leap, a celebration of his nature, his life and his work. My favourite of the thanksgivings offered up on that day ran as follows: 'From all the chauffeurs and builders on this planet, we thank the Lord for the blessed opportunity to travel, to restore, and to love.' Quaint, appropriate and profound, it sticks in my heart.

Leap had been given the kiss of life. Its revival had touched people from near and far, and as the focus of so much positive energy (I write this on Ascension Day) it seems not impossible to those whose minds have open windows that some sort of impetus was at work that propelled it towards its own salvation, when Peter was no longer there to implement it. How otherwise can one account for the arrival on the scene not of some hotelier, some magnate in search of social stature, some insensitive moderniser fancying the site, but of Seán, Anne and Ciara?

Seán Ryan and Anne Callanan are both very much involved in the artistic life of Ireland. Anne is well known as a teacher of traditional Irish dance, and runs her own school of dance at nearby Nenagh. Ciara, seven years old when I first met her, has a passion for dancing and already shows signs of a real talent. To watch her dance is to witness an embodiment of grace and gaiety; just what Leap needs. She loves her home, and was baptised in the chapel at Leap; an act of faith on the part of her parents, who are convinced that no evil spirits now inhabit it. They had difficulty in finding a priest who was prepared to conduct the ceremony, but eventually succeeded, and a beautiful service was held, during which candles set in the still glassless window recess that served as the altar are said to have remained unextinguished although a wind blew at the time.

Seán seems to be so exactly the perfect person to own and to restore Leap that I find it hard to believe that his arrival here was not another of those meaningful coincidences that have occurred from time to time in this story. He has three attributes that will enhance and revive it: he is a performing artist, a builder and a champion of all things Irish. As one of Ireland's best known and loved tin whistle players, who came to the fore in the 1970s, he has since then made a name for himself in the United States, in England and on the Continent. He comes from a very musical family. Initially he had intended to get a qualification in forestry but halfway through the training the call of music became so insistent that he changed tack completely, going off to London to earn a living on building sites and playing his music in public houses at nights. He was an immediate and resounding success. Returning to Ireland in 1979, he went to Galway, where traditional music was becoming increasingly popular. Soon he was in as great demand outside Ireland as within it, with increasing numbers of albums, cassettes and compact discs in circulation.

For all his expertise and celebrity, Seán is a modest and down-to-earth person; literally down to earth, for when he began to get to grips with the restoration work at Leap he started in the old cellars and dungeons, rebuilding the vaulting with his own hands in the traditional way, with skills learnt on the building sites of London. From there he has moved gradually upwards, augmenting the considerable amount of rebuilding already done by Peter Bartlett, and reorganising the interior in the most imaginative and appropriate manner. Seán and Anne have been kindness itself, escorting me all over those parts of the castle that are accessible, namely the keep and the adjoining south wing. Already, the place is well on its way to becoming a home. Séan has himself begun to replace the curly Gothic window-frames in exactly the old style, and he is opening up the old library, which was completely blocked by rubble. In Peter's time, an interesting thing occurred in connection with this. Two crates of books appeared mysteriously at the castle, many bearing the Leap bookplate. All were in good condition save for one damp one in the centre of each crate. Both of these concerned sites sacred to the Aboriginals of Western Australia, where Peter came from. The parallel histories of dispossession endured by two different races are obvious, and the message, whether accidental or contrived, uncannily apposite.

The huge first floor room, with the log fire blazing in the previously boarded-up fireplace that had so terrified little Patricia, now feels almost as if it had never been destroyed. A small gallery, an echo of the old one, occupies the thickness of the wall of the keep where it adjoins the south wing. I can imagine musicians playing there. Beyond it two bedrooms have been created, as well as a sauna and bathroom, the latter a far cry from Leap in my grandparents' time. They had one bath, put in after the Great War, and a selection of hip baths, filled with hot water from cans carried up two floors from the kitchen by the maids. After the family had returned from a day's foxhunting, four or five of these baths may well have had to be provided, in front of bedroom fires which the poor domestics had also to lay, light and keep going. Seán's new bathroom is almost on the site of the dreaded Muckle Hole, but such is the serenity, now, of that part of the castle that nothing more sinister than a shaving cut is likely to cause a blood-stain.

A true son of Ireland, Seán Ryan sees himself as custodian of a monument to his country's troubled past, even as he places stone upon fallen stone to ensure that it has a living future. The last time I saw him he was on his knees in the great hall at Leap. He was building a hearth, where once there had been one. He had entwined his initial and those of Anne and Ciara together in a traditional Celtic design as carved decoration on the stone chimney-piece. Here, near the entrance, there will be set the glowing embers of welcome. A far cry from the flame of the threatened cannon that admitted the English to the castle, a far cry from the bombs and dynamite that drove them out again. Seán and Anne will make this place a centre for many different aspects of Irish culture, as well as a home, sharing it with the Irish people.

Sadly, there is still some negative feeling about the whole Leap saga in the neighbourhood, though whether it is the Darby family or the place that evokes this is a mystery. One young man visiting Leap not long ago accepted a lift to Birr from two local girls in a car, after his own had broken down on the road near Leap. On the way, as they chatted and giggled about his misfortune, he let slip that his name was Darby. The girls fell silent. At the telephone box in the next village they stopped the car, telling the young man that he could ring for help from there. Who knows what was behind that little drama? Some dark memory?

Now is a time not for forgetting but for setting aside old grudges and fears to do with Leap. 'The Past', as Kath Walker has said, 'is all about us, and within', but the present is where we are, and the future is largely what we make it. Leap will always be a bulwark, but henceforth it will be a safe space where love can grow, where art can flourish, where music and dance will dispel any lingering aura of a turbulent history; a bulwark, now, against the insidious growth of materialism in our Western culture. It has been saved to good purpose.

11
An End and a Beginning

My legacy from Leap consists of a few objects and of what went on there that has affected my life. Like my cousins from that family, my Leap parent has had an enormous influence, and while I write mainly of my mother in this context I have ventured to touch on the characters of my aunts and uncle, whose children have told me of how their own lives were coloured in the same way. Darby grandchildren in Australia, Canada, Ireland and here in England all bear the mark of Leap.

My mother's childhood has already been described, and can be seen to have had a lasting effect on her future development. Her recollections of later years, up to the time of her marriage, reflect the enthusiasm of youth. She loved life and passed on this blessing to her children.

In 1909, when she was barely sixteen, Diana was presented at Court at Dublin Castle, because King Edward VII and Queen Alexandra would not be coming to Dublin the following year (in fact the year of the king's death). For her presentation my mother was, in her own words 'taken out of the schoolroom'. Her beautiful reddish-brown hair was put up, and court dresses were ordered from Paris for her and for her mother, who presented her. I have no doubt that they were of the finest; only the best was good enough for Milly, and subsequently for my mother, regardless of their financial position. There must have been a photograph of her, gone up in flames no doubt. Afterwards, the hair came down again and lessons were resumed. My mother enjoyed the spectacle but was, she said, glad to get back to her dogs and horses. There was no hurry to grow up in those days in families like the Darbys.

Diana adored animals, was interested in all country pursuits, and never lost her love of farming although she did not have a farm of her own for many years. She rode bravely to hounds, side-saddle of course. If the meet was some distance away from Leap she would take a pony and trap, starting very early, and would lead her hunter behind, so as not to tire herself or it by a long hack. Those winding lanes, down which a car must be driven with such caution, cannot have changed much during the twentieth century. I often think 'She would have known this tree, or that farm.' She fished all her life, and this became her passion, but she gave up shooting quite early on. Diana was well named – a true huntress, and goddess-like in appearance. Her wonderful legs were so long that her hunting boots were pronounced by their maker to be the longest woman's ones that he had ever made. As a girl she was regarded as a rare beauty, and her vitality and wit were added charms. 'Men cluster to me, like moths around a flame' sang Marlene Dietrich. They clustered round my mother for much of her life and were, inevitably, singed.

The eldest Miss Darby was no social butterfly. She joined the Red Cross during the early days of the Great War, training as a hospital nurse. She told us that she was among the few whom the commandant of the hospital would take onto the troopships when they came into harbour full of wounded soldiers, since she could be relied upon not to faint.[1] It was during leave from her duties towards the end of the war that my parents met at a party and very shortly afterwards became engaged.

Diana's marriage to my father, Edward Mark Philips, took place on 9 January 1919. The war was only just over, the Armistice having been signed a bare two months before the event. There was considerable unrest in Ireland, following the republican success in the general election of December 1918, but such was my father's infatuation for my mother that it is not once mentioned in his almost daily letters to her before the marriage. The wedding group was photographed on the front steps of the castle, framed by the Batty Langley doorway. Milly looks very modish and elegant in a dashing toque, Jonathan is slim and smart in the morning dress that was subsequently burnt, but looks gloomy: he was losing his favourite child. Horatio, who only managed to get leave at the last moment, wore his Irish Guards service dress for the occasion, and stands next to fifteen-year-old Patricia, who was the bridesmaid. My Aunt Cis stands on her left. Diana was a grave and stately bride, in a wedding dress made of cream Lyons brocade with a sunburst design in the weave. The material had been given to her by a neighbour in Ireland who had lost her fiancé in the Boer War with the wedding all planned.[2] The photographer, summoned from Dublin to

1 Blood did not disconcert my mother. I have forever in my mind's eye a picture of her during the last war disembowelling a hare for 'jugging', clad in a white, floating négligé and pink feathered mules.

2 It was just after the Second World War that I wore the same dress for my marriage.

record the occasion also took photographs of the castle from both sides, and these were the last ones ever to be taken of the house as a family home. Three years later it was a ruin.

Diana must have loved Leap, for during the early years of her marriage she was constantly returning there, as my father's anxious love letters testify. They reveal a man who is not entirely sure of his wife. My guess is that she enjoyed keeping him on his toes: her father's daughter, she liked power. That she was very much in love with her charismatic Englishman is not in doubt, but nor is the fact that she would never have settled at home in Ireland after the war, and marriage would have been, in that family, the only escape. More pragmatic than romantic (though she loved romantic situations and surroundings) Diana would have weighed up the advantages of the match rather than entering into it blindly, delighted as she doubtless was by Eddie's charm, good looks and wit. At nearly forty-one, he was already some way up the ladder of a prosperous career, was well born, kind and a keen sportsman, particularly as regards horses. All the girls loved Eddie, but it was Diana who had caught him, to the joy of both families.

My mother took after her father in that she was autocratic, quick-tempered and practical. She was a loving but rather alarming mother. Possessed of an enormous capacity for enjoyment and a bubbling sense of fun, she nevertheless created round her the kind of tension that she had known herself in her childhood. There were constant rows, which to her were, I suppose, the norm, but were unsettling to any child within earshot. I once heard her shouting to my father 'One day I shall kick over the traces' and it was not until I came across those very words in one of Milly's novels[3] that I realised that she may have heard her mother use them. The image of our adored mother snapping her harness and bolting away was a permanent anxiety to me.

It is obvious that Diana's experience of married life as lived by her parents had accustomed her to the expectation of almost daily discord, but there was one big difference in our household from that of Leap. My mother was determined to be the boss, and to do what she liked. She had no intention of becoming the underdog – her mother's role. She was warm and kind by nature, but was herself the victim not of a bullying husband but of an example of domestic behaviour on the part of her parents from which she could not break free. Treated as a boy from

3 *Anthropoid Apes* (1909), p. 288.

infancy, she, the most feminine of women, remained trapped in a male role; an incongruity which her three husbands (she outlived them all) at first found irresistible. Later, they had to fight to retain their own masculinity, not always with success, as my mother's extravagance and independent ways ate into their resources and sapped their pride. If they complained, she would fly into a fury. This was an unhappy legacy of the charged, hostile atmosphere that prevailed in that powerful place, Leap. My Aunt Cecily, too, was prone to fits of rage, and she also needed to dominate, but she was deceptively petite and almost kittenish with men, not a Valkyrie, like my mother. Uncle Horatio, a kind and loving man, cursed and shouted at his family just as his father had, but it was pure theatre and nobody minded. My Aunt Patricia, by nature more sensitive than her older sisters, was affected in a different way by her family background. As the youngest child, often made to feel that she was in the way, she was always nervous, and was for the rest of her life terrified of doing the wrong thing. In 1925, as I have already mentioned, Patricia married, for love, a clever and handsome naval lieutenant, Uncle Douglas Prentice.[4] He wore an eyeglass with aplomb, and served with distinction in the Second World War. As a naval officer's wife, it was my aunt's duty to observe the stringent conventions of the Senior Service, and this she did superbly, but she was haunted by anxiety about what people thought. This was frustrating for her children, much as they loved and admired her. We all loved her. I sometimes wonder whether, had she married some more congenial man than my grandfather, a fulfilled and appreciated Milly might not have displayed the same perceptive charm that radiated from my happily married Aunt Patricia, but without Patricia's anxieties. These almost certainly stemmed from her early life.

There is no doubt that Leap, that stronghold of passions, has left its imprint on Darby descendants until the present day. I am speaking of what has come down to us genetically as well as what has shaped us from that potent environment. All my generation of Darby descendants acknowledge that they have been influenced in positive and negative ways by what befell our respective Darby parent, and back beyond that. We have all felt the backwash from that flood of intense emotions and have been, to a greater or lesser degree, empowered or incapacitated by it. Our own children may well have been influenced, too,

4 Uncle Douglas was a 'sensitive'. On first seeing Leap, he identified it with a dream he had had of the place, years earlier, in which he had seen it roofless.

though obviously to a smaller extent, as other inherited or induced tendencies have intervened.

For those of us who are intent on bringing the past to life, objects play a fascinating part. They can trigger recollection, helping us to understand who we are, and why.

Some clairvoyant people practise what is known as psychometry. This consists in handling an object and divining something of its provenance. In a sense, that is what we all do when we consider family possessions, large or small, left behind by the dead, but it is memory rather than divination that usually activates our responses. Each artefact that I have inherited vibrates with associations, particularly when I touch it. My mother's belongings, perhaps understandably, evoke the most poignant reactions of all. Her firm, competent grasp haunts my hesitant one when I wield what were her kitchen utensils. Her hats, beautifully hand made, I had imagined would stand me in good stead for life, but her face inhabits them so decisively that it is mine which is ghostly when I put them on. Her immensely long, narrow shoes, of which I treasure one particularly characteristic pair, evoke the sound of her firm tread down corridors; unforgettable to the inmates of her house, family or staff, who, upon hearing them, felt impelled to spring up and engage in some useful activity. Newspapers hastily abandoned, books kicked beneath sofas, letters stowed under jerseys, these were the equivalent of the RAF's 'scramble' response to a call to duty. Woe betide the cook whose novelette was discovered in the meat safe! In this matter my mother was literally following in her father's footsteps; the sound of his boots on the stone floors and cobbled yards at Leap would have had exactly the same galvanic effect on any idle underling in his path.

I have one object that was my grandfather's. It is a handsome silver rose bowl, presented to him in 1901 by the North Tipperary and King's County Farming Society at their annual fatstock show, bearing both his name and that of his prizewinning Aberdeen Angus bull, Magus. Ely territory remained, as the poet O'Heedrin had remarked in O'Carroll days, a land of cattle. My hands enfold Jonathan's long slender ones whenever I hold the rose bowl, and I envisage his barely concealed pride on receiving it as the crowd claps and the bunting flaps languidly in the almost inevitable rain. Surely this trophy would have stood permanently on the sideboard at Leap, and has survived only because it had been providentially removed from Leap with some of the other silver before the fire. To me it is a chalice, holding all that my grandfather stood for.

The few things I have which were my grandmother's are particularly evocative because of the great affinity that I feel for her. When I pick up her silver looking-glass I imagine her small hand beneath my large one as she inspects the work of her lady's maid on her elaborate coiffure, but it is Milly's jewellery box and the contents thereof that hold, for me, some of the most precious of family associations. Here I must employ my own memories, hearsay, and also to some degree the psychometrist's art. The purple morocco-leather box, previously mentioned in the Introduction to this book, was with her from her girlhood. Stout and foursquare like the keep of the castle she lived in, the lock is violated and the key gone. I have this treasure before me as I write. It smells musty. The dust within may well include particles of Leap dust. I see this little container, Milly's secret place, as a microcosm of the macrocosm that was Milly. Its importance to her is indicated by her having taken it with her on the flight from the castle in March 1922. The contents have a kind of chronology. The earliest object must be the fragment of a greetings card; a delicate engraving, showing a bird on the wing and bearing the message 'Mildred H. Gordon Dill from Mother. Nov. 20 1882'. Milly was fourteen and eight months. Was the box a Confirmation present? Then there is the remains of a seed-pearl necklace, the kind of thing young girls wore in those days, and a collection of little brooches and tie pins, some clearly meant for a hunting stock, and one of Egyptian design which may have been a gift from her friend Sir Flinders Petrie, the celebrated Egyptologist who carried out excavations on the pyramids and temples of the Nile from the 1890s onwards. My mother recalled that he had given Milly an ankh: this has disappeared. Perhaps, at the time when 'the Curse of Tutankhamen' was the talk of the day, she thought it might bring bad luck and got rid of it. A pair of imitation diamond brooches, designed to be worn together, I have divided, giving one to Ciara and one to Milly and Jonathan's great-great-granddaughter, Louisa Wedderburn, hoping that these twin objects may foster an affinity between the two girls. 'Only connect...' said E. M. Forster on the title page of his own story of a house and its inhabitants, *Howards End*.

Milly's calling-card, also mentioned at the start of this story, is tucked into one corner of the box, a reminder of her lost status. She would have carried some of these in a small wallet specially designed to hold them when she set out in her pony and trap several afternoons a week to pay calls on her neighbours, especially any new arrivals of the correct social stature. Time must have hung heavy for a writer who had been forbidden to exercise her craft, and this social duty, which allowed Milly to drive her trotting ponies, would have been a welcome diversion. Patricia recalled being roped in to accompany her mother on these expeditions, which were generally tedious for a child of that generation, who was expected to be seen and not heard. In the same compartment of the box is a reading-glass on a black cord, probably belonging to my grandmother's later life, but a hunt button, bearing an interlaced monogram that I am unable to disentangle[5] harks back to her hunting days at Leap. Several periodical wrappers addressed to Johnnie Minchin at Cheltenham boys' school suggests that my grandmother sent this cherished grandson a magazine at intervals. An account from a Sussex newspaper of her mother's 102nd birthday in 1925 is carefully preserved with another from the *Daily Sketch*, together with press announcements of Molly's death and funeral in that same year, and a little scrawled note, written, it seems, by an almost totally blind person, reading 'Love to my dearest Milly from Mother'. I have one such missive from my mother, in her ninety-seventh year. One cannot bring oneself to discard what was written with such effort, especially when the word 'love' is in the text.

Comic relief is present in the form of a letter from an old Leap employee, dated 11 September 1926, which contains the observation that 'The governor [Grandfather] seems to be very hard to deal with these days'[6] and requests that my grandmother send him a sum of money demanded by Grandfather for rabbits that the writer had shot in the Leap grounds and sold. In this way, Jonathan Darby could be paid off. Granny seems to have agreed to this quaint transaction, for on the back of the letter is a receipt signed by the writer for £20, 'from Mrs Darby'. How often Milly must have intervened in situations where her husband was behaving outrageously!

The latest item in the box is a Christmas label with a tinselly tag bearing the legend 'Mother, with love from Eddie', my father. I remember what the present was: a woollen scarf in two shades of grey, to protect that wheezing chest. Childhood, harked back to, throws up precise fragments of a hazy whole, much as an exhumed mosaic pavement sometimes reveals little perfect pieces of pattern in a welter of rubble. Less than a month later Milly died in hospital.

5 The West Meath Hunt seems the most likely reading.

6 An observation borne out by several newspaper descriptions of law suits with his erstwhile neighbours during the Twenties.

The only other thing my grandmother preserved in her jewellery box brings the wheel of Darby history round full circle. At the very bottom, hidden under the fitted tray, is a bundle of carefully folded, yellowing newspaper accounts of the burning. In one of these the story of Finola and the Captain features prominently. Once more the legend rears its head. I have no doubt that Milly believed it absolutely, and that in naming all but her first child O'Carroll she was reinforcing what she saw as a vital link, enriching and ennobling the family. That she probably invented a great deal of the tale would be no obstacle to belief in it: a characteristic inherited to a quite alarming degree by my mother.

Cross-fertilisation makes for a composite species. The Darbys wanted the O'Carroll connection for their own nourishment, to strengthen their association with the country to which they had come as unwelcome settlers; in short, to make them feel more Irish. Since Milly and her children never questioned the legend, we of my generation have digested it so completely as to feel that the O'Carrolls are part of our make-up. Nurture has implanted in our minds what nature may or may not have sown in the body. Those of us with O'Carroll in our name or consciousness feel the confluence of our known and posited lineage; an entwinement as in Celtic art.

As yet, no facts have been exhumed to render the Finola story undeniably fictional. If that were to happen in my lifetime, I do not think I would be aware of the amputation, although I would know that the operation had taken place.[7] In this as in many other Leap matters, I am content to be where I am: the suspension of disbelief frees me to live 'as if', which is to take wing on the hypothesis of my choice, and hope it will carry me in the general direction of the truth.

In old age, no longer anyone's child, one sometimes seems to catch a liberating glimpse of one's essential identity, and it is in such moments that I feel detached enough to glory in the fact of Leap, together with its fictions; to stand apart from it and see it in its entirety – history, legends, ghosts and all – as a battered, many-faceted jewel that belongs not to any one family, but to Ireland. Family ownership of the castle in the past gave power to the owners, whether Irish nobles, squabbling for possession, or English settlers.[8] In both these cases, power was used to

7 Amputees frequently assert that this is the case.

8 A letter dated 1867, pathetic in hindsight, from Horatio, younger brother of William Henry Darby, to Lord Rosse, contains the assertion 'that Property belongs to those who possess it, and it is absurd, now, to talk of "Ireland for the Irish".'

dominate. This is no longer so. The fire did away with all that, the one good thing to come out of that act of vandalism. Leap revived begins a new existence under an unselfish proprietor for the good of all. It is still a centre of power, the power of love and of art, each of which becomes magnified in being shared. A home it has always been and will remain. Smoke from the hearth of Leap, curling up from the chimney into the soft Irish air, proclaims its warm heart. The two words, hearth and heart, from the same root, mean almost the same thing.

Ciara, a flesh and blood girl, will one day become the heir to Leap Castle, like legendary Finola O'Carroll. I hope that she finds true love in less hazardous circumstances than her predecessor, and will live happily at Leap for many years. I imagine the great hall of the castle lit up on her wedding day and filled with the sound of music, as it was on that morning when I first revisited it after so many years.

At this time of a new beginning, I have reached the end of my tale. The threads of history, of hearsay, of recollection and of conjecture are woven into curious garments to clothe the host of fading figures who lived at Leap down the ages. Full of holes, often ill-fitting, the clothing has, I hope, given substance to that procession, particularly to those at the tail end of it who have come into clearer focus; those I can actually remember. As for the castle itself, which stones stood upon which, for what reason and for how long, may never be known. Its potent presence is made up of elements that are largely indefinable, however hard people may try to analyse its heart-stopping impact and curious charm. That it will never be wholly devoid of brooding menace somehow adds to the attraction; it is a kind of Heathcliffe in stone. It could have been left to moulder away like some ruined crusader castle out in the desert. How long, I wonder, would it have retained its spirit? That spirit could have been all but extinguished by unsympathetic restoration, had the castle fallen into the hands of insensitive people. Thank God that it was rescued by Peter Bartlett, whose vision, alas! was never realised, and that it was saved for the second time by Seán Ryan, also a man with a dream.

The last two lines of a love sonnet by the poet Michael Drayton[9] ring in my mind whenever I rejoice in the small miracle of Leap's salvation:

> Now, if thou would'st, when all have given him over,
> From death to life thou might'st him yet recover.

9 1563–1631.

Appendices

APPENDIX I

National Dress

These Chieftains and their attendant nobles wore, by the Middle Ages, clothes that were both practical and elegant, consisting of a knee length woven shift and a mantle, or *brat*, of thicker material, often in a rich colour, with embroidery at the hem and corners and sometimes crafted metal work to hold it down in a wind. It was secured by a brooch of a convoluted Celtic design, and the overall effect was more akin to ancient Roman military dress than to the Norman look of the invaders. Women, too, wore the tunic-like undergarment. In both cases an ornate girdle or belt would be worn round the waist, and sometimes this shift, or *leine*, as it was called, had a hood attached. Dressier members of the clan might sport a fringe around the hem. The women also wore a cloak, which you could either flaunt for effect or wrap round you for warmth, and the richer ones would have worn dresses. Leather sandals completed the ensemble for those who could afford them. The large-framed, golden-haired O'Carroll nobles must have looked splendid in this attire, though the poorer relations wore less becoming and coarser garments; baggy breeches are sometimes to be seen in old pictures. Helmets in a variety of shapes were sometimes worn for fighting and a rather stylish conical cap features in some early illustrations. Peasants went bareheaded.

Later, fashions became more elaborate as textile techniques improved, with more tailored garments, including tight trews and jackets, showing European influence. Garments became even more richly embroidered and trimmed, when luxury materials from the Near East became available. From the fourteenth century onwards, the English tried to force the Irish to abandon their ethnic dress and Henry VIII actually legislated against certain garments, but those not yet subjugated ignored the edict.

APPENDIX 2

Wild Geese

There were very large Irish contingents in the French and Spanish forces, which had Irish regiments and even brigades, and smaller groups, too, in other European armies. At first these contingents contained a mixture of officers and other ranks – some of James II's regiments had escaped intact after the disaster of the Boyne defeat. Subsequently, however, it was usually only the gentry who emigrated in this way, as most were understandably too proud to demean themselves by becoming the servants of their oppressors, without rights and committed to menial work on the land or with horses. In the Spanish army there were seven Irish regiments, all save one with Irish names – the Dublin Dragoons and the Waterford, Hibernia, Ultonia, Limerick and Irlanda Regiments. We cannot be sure how many of the O'Carroll Wild Geese were of Ely. A Capitan Antonio Caroli is in the 1721 list of the Dublin Dragoons, while the Waterford Regiment had Capitan Andres Carroll and Cadete Renaldo Carroll on its strength in 1716 and 1731 respectively. Renaldo seems to have transferred to the Irish regiment in 1733, since he is on record as saying that he had come from Ireland to join his uncle, Juan Trant, tenente and paymaster to the regiment.

In the French forces there were at least four Irish regiments, forming the French Irish Brigade, and there were other Irish units that fought either independently or alongside them. Under Marshal de Catinat in 1693 at the Battle of Marsaglia against the Italians (allies of King William), the Irish troops helped to secure victory by a combination of wiliness and valour. During this battle, Brigadier Francis O'Carroll died a hero's death after a tremendous charge by the Irish, who had lured the enemy within range by feigning surrender. A worthy end for a disinherited pawn of fortune.

It must have been very lonely and confusing for those young men, many of whom had probably never been more than fifty miles from home, to embrace an alien culture. They were more than mercenaries, they were for the most part landed gentry in search of new roots while retaining their proud identity in service to a new monarch.

APPENDIX 3

Letter from John Nelson Darby to his Brother Horatio

5 October 1835

My dear Horatio

I cannot help longing that you should be partaker of the blessings we enjoy tho' I do not mean there are no trials in them but we are taught to respect them and they serve to keep one humble. What led to this was our labours now drawing round and so near you and many having decided of our way of thinking about things. The Clarkes and Walshes & others coming decidedly not among a despised remnant as weak as you please but seeking to be separate from evil and serve the Lord therewith by regular preaching I trust? at Birr [indecipherable] & Kane & Walsh Park now & I believe at Castle Willington & the neighbourhood. I admit the weakness of their instrument but our experience has been that wherever they have been weakest if humble the most blessing and that the very thing the Church wants is to have to [indecipherable] from man to cease from having confidence in the flesh, this is not pleasant to the flesh to have but 12 to listen. This has been the case with us when all I believe have been brought to the Lord & are now breaking bread together & more may win others among them tho' of men young & not 11 miles thence we have have had 150 or 200 sometimes to hear as constantly 100 devoted Christians the[indecipherable] the [indecipherable] when I am not aware that by the preaching one person has been brought to the Lord thus we learn tho' [indecipherable] does not hurt in the flesh nor [indecipherable] the day of small things [indecipherable] get a principle right in whatever measures and you must find God helping tho' he may exercise his patience. The world's all [indecipherable]. I rejoice when you say pray God to make me more faithful to him. This is what we want for this only abides in its fruit and all the rest perishes in the using. May you find the comfort and joy of living thoroughly out for the Lord. I am sorry you did not see Arthur. It was want of perfect acquaintance on his part with [indecipherable] partly and ill arrangement as to the rest his simple Godliness tells by a most blameless & devoted life with God tho' a man of no pretensions & other [indecipherable] in these days of [indecipherable]. I am at present at Cork where we have a house for the Saints Arthur having half it is a good large one and very soon I shall have indeed I might say now I have a plan to you if you should be inclined to pay us a visit might it in [indecipherable]. I am waited for & must be off. Pray the Lord to make you very faithful ever my dear Hoo.

Yr very affectionate brother JND

APPENDIX 4

Admiral George Darby

Admiral George cannot be fitted into the Darby family tree as either the uncle or great-uncle of Henry because he cannot reasonably be placed in the generations to which he would supposedly have belonged. As to documentary evidence, George's will names several of his closest relations whose names and descriptions are inconsistent with those of the Darbys of Leap. Nor does the will actually mention any of the Leap Darbys, with the exception of a codicil containing a gift to Henry and there is no acknowledgement of any family relationship between them.

The only basis for the belief that George was the uncle of Henry is a letter of 1781 from George to Lord Sandwich in which he explicitly claims kinship with 'my relation Captain Darby',[1] leaving the exact nature of that relationship, perhaps deliberately, vague. George was always reticent about his origins (another reason for concluding that he was not the son of a Darby of Leap) and was described as being 'without the assistance of patronage',[2] a serious deficiency in the eighteenth and early nineteenth century Royal Navy. Hints or claims of kinship with the Darbys of Leap would have been of mutual benefit to George, securing his social acceptability, and to Henry, giving him friends in high places.

1 George Darby to Lord Sandwich, 20 June 1781, in *The Private Papers of John, Earl of Sandwich, First Lord of the Admiralty 1771–1782*, ed. G. R. Barnes and J. H. Owen, vol. 4 (Navy Records Society, 1938), p. 45.
2 Ibid. pp. 31–2.

APPENDIX 5

Loyal Addresses

(Excerpt from *The Tribune*, 22 July 1880)

ADDRESS PRESENTED BY HIS TENANTRY TO J. C. DARBY ESQ, LEAP CASTLE, ON HIS TAKING POSSESSION OF HIS ESTATES

Dear Sir,

We, the undersigned, beg to offer you our sincere and hearty congratulations on your entering into the possession of your Estates, and coming to reside in the house of your fathers. We have long looked forward to this day with joyful expectation, and desire to tender you, Mrs. Darby, and each member of your family our most cordial welcome.

Your respected father's memory is still cherished in our affectionate regards, particularly as we recollect the many years of his young life which he spent in our midst, and the many deeds of kindness which endeared him to us all, and we trust to find in you, his honoured representative, the worthy son of a worthy father.

In the many changes and vicissitudes of life we sincerely trust that the relationship of Landlord and Tenant many always exist between us on most cordial terms – our mutual interests being so closely united together- and that nothing may ever arise to lessen your confidence in us.

Hoping that God's good hand may guide and prosper all that you do, that His blessing may rest on each member of your family, and that our connection may be a long and happy one,

We have the honour to be

Your obedient Servants,

(signed on behalf of the tenants)

SAMUEL HYDE, CLK
GERALD RYALL
THOMAS ARDILL
ROBERT ARDILL
GEORGE ARMSTRONG
DANIEL BERGIN
WM. CARRY
THEOPHILUS WALLACE JNR
JOHN JOHNSON

REPLY (in the same edition of the newspaper)

Mr. Hyde, Tenants and Friends,

I owe you my sincerest thanks for this address, which reveals to me the kindly feeling that has existed, and I hope will ever exist, between my family and the tenants on the Leap Estate.

Now that I am entering on my duties as a landlord, I hope that nothing in the way of Legislation may sever that bond of union. Also, I trust that I shall be able, to the best of my ability, to further your interests in your occupations and improvements, though you all know the disadvantages, incumbrances, and dilapidations which I now inherit with the Property.

I am sure I and my mother, and the rest of the family, feel much touched and gratified by your most kindly remembrance of my dear father, whose kindness I know won many a heart; all the more, too, as he was entirely ignored as the son and heir.

My mother and the rest of the family join in thanking you all, from the least to the greatest, for all the kind wishes you have expressed; and I know they will do all in their power to show sympathy with and relieve those on my property who need it, and I hope they may long be spared to do so....

Again thanking you,

I remain,
Yours most truly,
J. C. DARBY

APPENDIX 6

The Ruin: Early Transactions

After Sam Spencer's death, his wife decided to sell Leap, in the early 1970s. According to my aunt Cecily (Cis), Jonathan's second daughter, writing to George Cunningham, 'the two Darby boys' (Horatio's two surviving sons, Fionn and Christopher) wanted it and left her to negotiate with Mrs Spencer's solicitor, Mr Kennedy. It then transpired that 'an English speculative builder' had arrived and offered her £2,250. It seems that Mrs Spencer 'expected the Darbys to give more'. Aunt Cis concluded that had she had a few days more she could have raised £250 extra on behalf of Fionn and Christopher, but then heard that Mrs Spencer had 'closed with the builder'. It was subsequently bought by Victor Mitchell of Mount Butler who in turn sold it to Peter Gerrard. He found an American buyer who reneged on the deal. It was at this point that Peter Bartlett turned up to see the home of his Bannon (O'Banon) ancestors, heard it was for sale and bought it in 1974.

APPENDIX 7

Names and Reigns of Leap Chieftains

John d. 1407
Ferganainm 1532–36
Donald 1536–38
Ferganainm 1538–41
Thady (and Charles) 1541–53/4
William 1554–81
John 1581–82
Charles 1582–1600
John 1600. Chief in name only; evicted by 1667

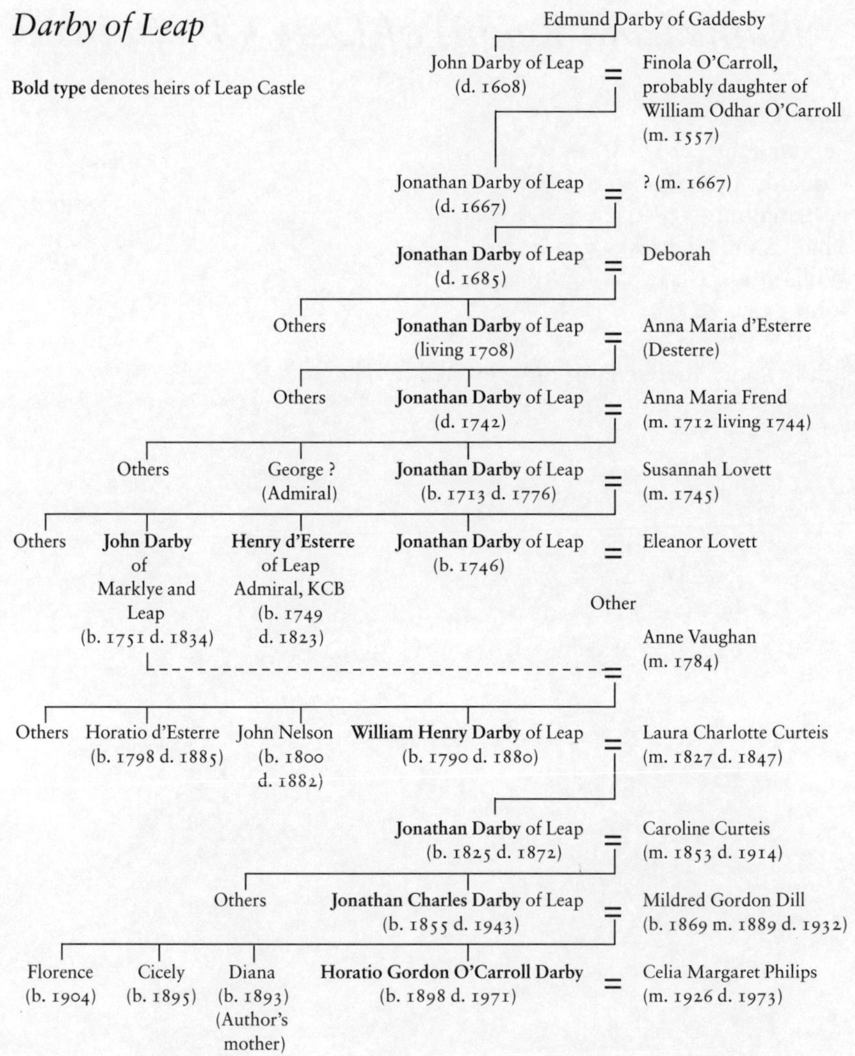
Darby of Leap
Bold type denotes heirs of Leap Castle
Edmund Darby of Gaddesby
John Darby of Leap (d. 1608)
Finola O'Carroll, probably daughter of William Odhar O'Carroll (m. 1557)
Jonathan Darby of Leap (d. 1667)
? (m. 1667)
Jonathan Darby of Leap (d. 1685)
Deborah
Others
Jonathan Darby of Leap (living 1708)
Anna Maria d'Esterre (Desterre)
Others
Jonathan Darby of Leap (d. 1742)
Anna Maria Frend (m. 1712 living 1744)
Others
George ? (Admiral)
Jonathan Darby of Leap (b. 1713 d. 1776)
Susannah Lovett (m. 1745)
Others
John Darby of Marklye and Leap (b. 1751 d. 1834)
Henry d'Esterre of Leap Admiral, KCB (b. 1749 d. 1823)
Jonathan Darby of Leap (b. 1746)
Eleanor Lovett
Other
Anne Vaughan (m. 1784)
Others
Horatio d'Esterre (b. 1798 d. 1885)
John Nelson (b. 1800 d. 1882)
William Henry Darby of Leap (b. 1790 d. 1880)
Laura Charlotte Curteis (m. 1827 d. 1847)
Jonathan Darby of Leap (b. 1825 d. 1872)
Caroline Curteis (m. 1853 d. 1914)
Others
Jonathan Charles Darby of Leap (b. 1855 d. 1943)
Mildred Gordon Dill (b. 1869 m. 1889 d. 1932)
Florence (b. 1904)
Cicely (b. 1895)
Diana (b. 1893) (Author's mother)
Horatio Gordon O'Carroll Darby (b. 1898 d. 1971)
Celia Margaret Philips (m. 1926 d. 1973)

Map of the District

Courtesy of the Cultural Tourism Centre

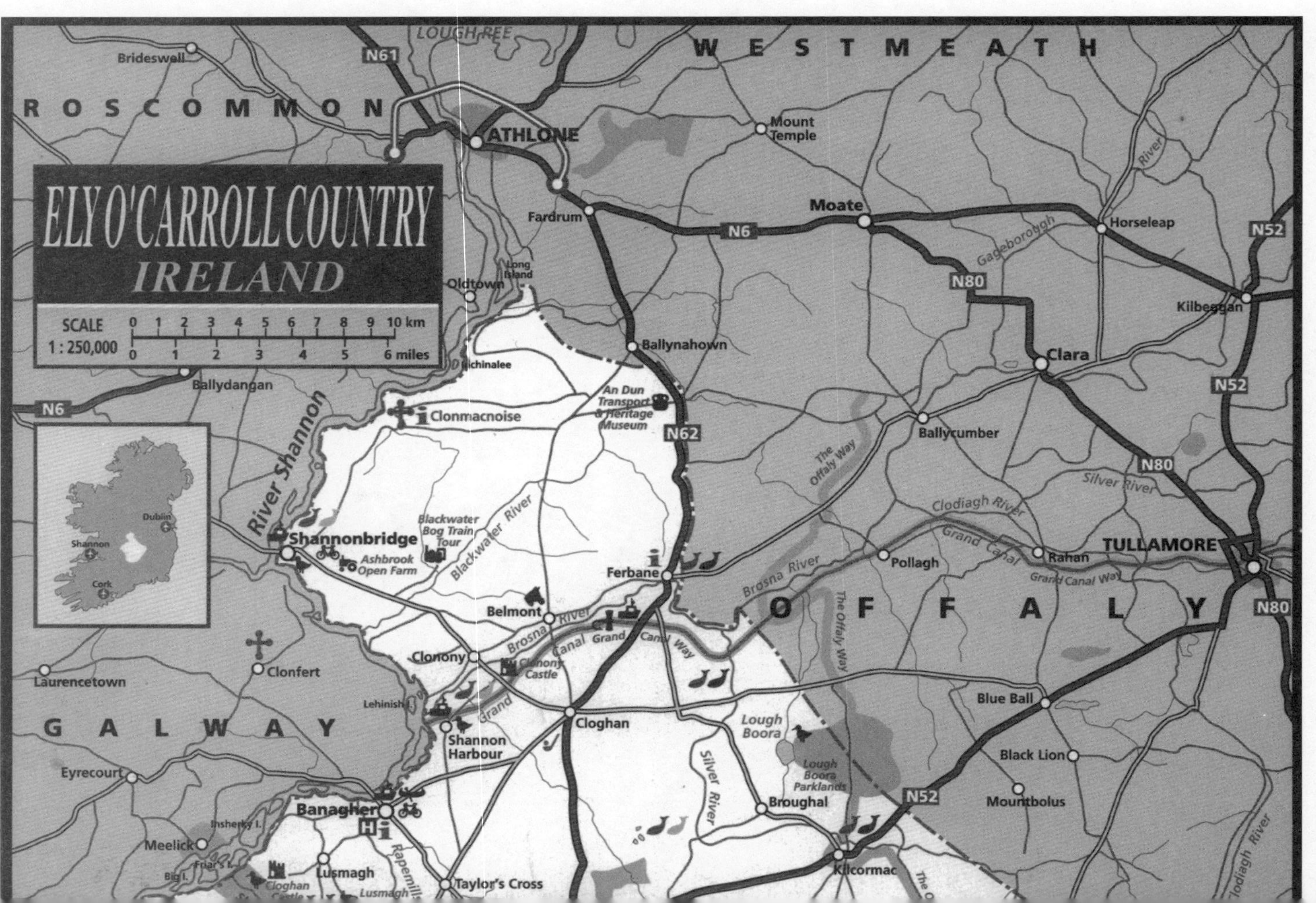

ELY O'CARROLL COUNTRY
IRELAND
SCALE
1 : 250,000
0 1 2 3 4 5 6 7 8 9 10 km
0 1 2 3 4 5 6 miles
ROSCOMMON
WESTMEATH
OFFALY
GALWAY
LOUGH REE
N61
N6
N80
N52
N62
ATHLONE
TULLAMORE
Brideswell
Mount Temple
Moate
Horseleap
Kilbeggan
Fardrum
Long Island
Oldtown
Ballynahown
Clara
Ballydangan
Clonmacnoise
An Dun Transport & Heritage Museum
Ballycumber
River Shannon
Shannonbridge
Ashbrook Open Farm
Blackwater Bog Train Tour
Blackwater River
Ferbane
The Offaly Way
Silver River
Clodiagh River
Grand Canal
Pollagh
Rahan
Grand Canal Way
Brosna River
Belmont
Clonony
Clonony Castle
Clonfert
Laurencetown
Lehinish I.
Cloghan
Shannon Harbour
Lough Boora
Lough Boora Parklands
Blue Ball
Black Lion
Mountbolus
Eyrecourt
Banagher
Broughal
Insherky I.
Meelick
Friar's I.
Big I.
Lusmagh
Cloghan Castle
Rapemills
Taylor's Cross
Kilcormac
Dublin
Shannon
Cork

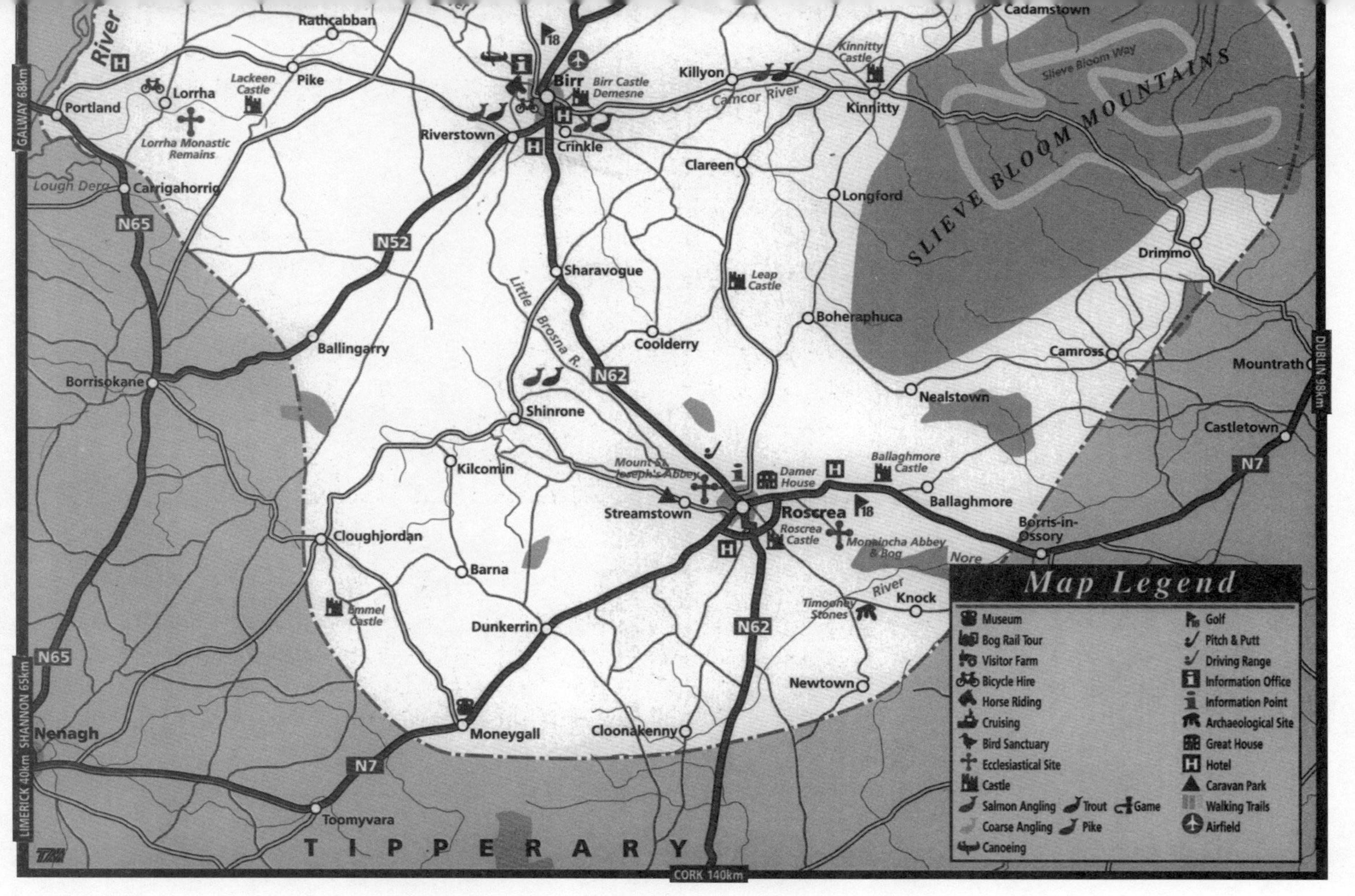
Map Legend
Museum
Bog Rail Tour
Visitor Farm
Bicycle Hire
Horse Riding
Cruising
Bird Sanctuary
Ecclesiastical Site
Castle
Salmon Angling
Trout
Game
Coarse Angling
Pike
Canoeing
Golf
Pitch & Putt
Driving Range
Information Office
Information Point
Archaeological Site
Great House
Hotel
Caravan Park
Walking Trails
Airfield
DUBLIN 98km
CORK 140km
LIMERICK 40km
SHANNON 65km
GALWAY 68km
SLIEVE BLOOM MOUNTAINS
Slieve Bloom Way
TIPPERARY
Cadamstown
Rathcabban
Pike
Portland
Lorrha
Lackeen Castle
Lorrha Monastic Remains
Lough Derg
Carrigahorrig
Birr
Birr Castle Demesne
Riverstown
Crinkle
Killyon
Camcor River
Kinnitty Castle
Kinnitty
Clareen
Longford
Drimmo
Leap Castle
Sharavogue
Little Brosna R.
Boheraphuca
Coolderry
Camross
Mountrath
Ballingarry
Borrisokane
Shinrone
Nealstown
Castletown
Kilcomin
Mount St. Joseph's Abbey
Damer House
Ballaghmore Castle
Ballaghmore
Streamstown
Roscrea
Roscrea Castle
Monaincha Abbey & Bog
Borris-in-Ossory
Nore
Cloughjordan
Barna
Timoney Stones
River
Knock
Emmel Castle
Dunkerrin
Newtown
Nenagh
Moneygall
Cloonakenny
Toomyvara
N7
N52
N62
N65

Select Bibliography

Attwater, Donald, *The Penguin Dictionary of Saints*, 2nd ed. revised Catherine Rachel John, Penguin, 1983.

Bence-Jones, Mark, *Twilight of the Ascendancy*, Constable, London, 1993.

Connolly, S. J. (ed.), *The Oxford Companion to Irish History*, Oxford University Press, 1998.

Cooke, Thomas L., *Cooke's History of Birr*, Dublin, 1875.

Crowl, Philip A., *The Intelligent Traveller's Guide to Historic Ireland*, Gill and MacMillan, Dublin, 1990.

De Paor, Liam, *Portrait of Ireland,* Rainbow Publications, Wicklow, 1985.

Feehan, John, *The Landscape of Slieve Bloom*, The Blackwater Press, Dublin, 1979.

Fingall, Elizabeth, Countess of, *Seventy Years Young*, The Lilliput Press, Dublin, 1991.

Fisher, H. A. L., *A History of Europe*, Edward Arnold, London, 1937.

Foster, R. F. (ed.), *The Oxford History of Ireland*, Oxford University Press, 1992.

Godkin, James and John A. Walker, *The New Hand-Book of Ireland,* Dublin Steam Printing Company (n.d.).

Hennessy, Maurice N., *The Wild Geese: The Irish Soldier in Exile*, Sidgwick and Jackson, London, 1973.

Joyce, P. W., *A Child's History of Ireland,* Longman & Co., Dublin, 1910.

Ironside, H. A., *A Historical Sketch of the Brethren Movement*, Zondervan Publishing House, Grand Rapids, 1942.

Lalor, Brian, *Ireland: Blue Guide,* A. & C. Black, London, 1995, seventh edition.

'Merry, Andrew', 'An April Fool', from *Under One Cover,* London, Skeffington & Son, 1898.

'Merry, Andrew', *The Green Country,* Grant Richards, London, 1902.

'Merry, Andrew', *Paddy Risky,* Grant Richards, London, 1903.

'Merry, Andrew', *Anthropoid Apes, A Modern Novel,* Henry J. Drane, London, 1909.

'Merry, Andrew', *The Hunger,* Andrew Melrose, London, 1910.

Moody, T. W. and F. X. Martin (edd.), *The Course of Irish History,* The Mercier Press, Cork, 1978.

Nolan, William and Timothy P. O'Neill, *Offaly – History & Society: Interdisciplinary Essays on the History of an Irish County*, Geography Publications, Dublin, 1998.

Compiled by Caimin O'Brien and, P. David Sweetman, *Archaeological Inventory of County Offaly*, The Stationery Office, Dublin, 1997.

Ó hEithir, Breandán, *Pocket History of Ireland,* The O'Brien Press, Dublin, 1989.

Sitwell, Sacheverell, *Dance of the Quick and the Dead,* Faber & Faber, London, 1936.

Smith, Grover, 'Yeats, Gogarty, and The Leap Castle Ghost', from *Modern Irish Literature*, ed. Raymond J. Porter and James D. Brophy, Iona College Press, New York, 1972.

Wallace, Martin, *Famous Irish Writers,* Appletree Press, Belfast, 1995.

Yeats, W. B. (ed.), *Fairy and Folk Tales of the Irish Peasantry,* Walter Scott Ltd, London (n.d.).

Index